NEW DIRECTIONS FOR HIGHER EDUCATION

Martin Kramer
EDITOR-IN-CHIEF

Leveraging Resources Through Partnerships

Lawrence G. Dotolo
Virginia Tidewater Consortium for Higher Education and
Association for Consortium Leadership

John B. Noftsinger, Jr.
James Madison University and *Association for Consortium Leadership*

EDITORS

Number 120, Winter 2002

JOSSEY-BASS
San Francisco

#51279097

LEVERAGING RESOURCES THROUGH PARTNERSHIPS
Lawrence G. Dotolo, John B. Noftsinger, Jr. (eds.)
New Directions for Higher Education, no. 120
Martin Kramer, Editor-in-Chief

Microfilm copies of issues and articles are available in 16mm and 35mm, as well as microfiche in 105mm, through University Microfilms Inc., 300 North Zeeb Road, Ann Arbor, Michigan 48106-1346.

ISSN 0271-0560   electronic ISSN 1536-0741

NEW DIRECTIONS FOR HIGHER EDUCATION is part of The Jossey-Bass Higher and Adult Education Series and is published quarterly by Wiley Subscription Services, Inc., a Wiley company, at Jossey-Bass, 989 Market Street, San Francisco, California 94103-1741. Periodicals postage paid at San Francisco, California, and at additional mailing offices. Postmaster: Send address changes to New Directions for Higher Education, Jossey-Bass, 989 Market Street, San Francisco, California 94103-1741

New Directions for Higher Education is indexed in Current Index to Journals in Education (ERIC); Higher Education Abstracts.

SUBSCRIPTIONS cost $70 for individuals and $145 for institutions, agencies, and libraries. See ordering information page at end of book.

EDITORIAL CORRESPONDENCE should be sent to the Editor-in-Chief, Martin Kramer, 2807 Shasta Road, Berkeley, California 94708-2011.

Cover photograph and random dot by Richard Blair/Color & Light © 1990.

Jossey-Bass Web address: www.josseybass.com

Printed in the United States of America on acid-free recycled paper containing at least 20 percent postconsumer waste.

CONTENTS

EDITORS' NOTES

Cooperation has been an important aspect of higher education for many years. There have been partnerships involving such areas as purchasing, libraries, faculty development, international programs, television, workforce development, and economic development, to name a few. These partnerships have been easy for higher education policymakers to talk about as solutions but are deceivingly difficult to implement and manage. Currently, partnerships are an essential part of higher education, and they will become increasingly more important as institutions try to achieve more with limited resources. Most postsecondary institutions are involved in some kind of consortial arrangement with other institutions or are engaged in partnerships with organizations and agencies external to higher education. This volume provides vivid examples of partnerships that have proven to be beneficial and successful for all the participants. More important, it provides concrete implementation strategies for institutions seeking to establish alliances with other institutions of higher education or with outside organizations. The chapters address leveraging resources, K–12 partnerships, economic development, community development, workforce development, technology partnerships, library cooperation, partnerships to serve the military, group purchasing, interinstitutional faculty collaboration, television partnerships, cooperation in international programs, and assessing a consortium's effectiveness. The breadth of these topics indicates how widespread cooperation is among institutions, and the expert depth shared by the chapter authors is immensely helpful.

The chapter authors collectively possess more than 250 years of experience in working in cooperative settings, and many have been instrumental in developing and enhancing some of the most successful consortia in the United States. This volume will be helpful to groups or agencies seeking partnerships with higher education in determining which avenue is best for them to follow in establishing programs. For those who have chosen an avenue, this volume provides examples of proven and innovative implementation strategies.

At this critical juncture, it is clear that higher education leaders must expand their reach. This volume addresses the ways that institutions or consortia have had an impact on improving the lives of people socially, economically, culturally, and intellectually. Higher education has the opportunity and mission to be the focal point of establishing alliances and partnerships that affect entire communities—local, national, and international.

All of the chapter authors are members of the Association for Consortium Leadership, the national organization of consortia. The association offers those interested in partnership activities a wealth of information, including a directory of consortia in the United States and their activities, a listserv where important questions of cooperation are openly discussed, a newsletter, and an annual conference for members and nonmembers to share innovative programmatic models, ideas, and concerns. The association also maintains a list of consortium directors who are willing to serve as consultants to institutions considering cooperative arrangements. These resources and materials can be found on the Association for Consortium Leadership's Web site (http://www.acl.odu.edu).

We thank Nicola Beltz, secretary to the board of the Association for Consortium Leadership and assistant to the president of the Virginia Tidewater Consortium for Higher Education, for her invaluable assistance in managing this project with professionalism and care and keeping everyone on task.

Lawrence G. Dotolo
John B. Noftsinger Jr.
Editors

LAWRENCE G. DOTOLO is president of the Virginia Tidewater Consortium for Higher Education and also serves as the executive director of the Association for Consortium Leadership in Norfolk, Virginia.

JOHN B. NOFTSINGER, JR. is associate vice president of academic affairs for research and program innovation and executive director of the Valley of Virginia Partnership for Education at James Madison University in Harrisonburg, Virginia, president of the Shenandoah Valley Technology Council, and vice president of the Association for Consortium Leadership.

1

Consortial arrangements afford the opportunity for colleges and universities to leverage resources jointly so that the end result produces more than the member could have accomplished single-handedly.

Expanding Resources: Benefits to Colleges and Universities

Anneke J. Larrance

Most higher education administrators recognize that there is no longer a choice about whether to leverage resources. It is a given as the economic climate has become unfavorable in many states. Leveraging resources is not just about sharing or dividing resources; rather, it is the synergistic process of making more from what is available. For example, a group of professionals from the consortium of the Associated Colleges of the St. Lawrence Valley who work with multicultural students on their own campuses meet regularly. The consortium leverages their efforts by offering the staff professional opportunities for networking. In return, this group has spearheaded a recognition ceremony for scholarship among multicultural students, formed a parallel organization for multicultural students, and lobbied for additional state aid money. This is more than what the individual members could hope to accomplish on their own.

Leveraging resources is a process that creates growth and energy. A shared initiative today may save the consortium and member institutions money and can often pave the way to further collaboration that can expand learning opportunities, add value, or encourage growth.

There are short- and long-term benefits when resources are leveraged. The benefits range from the obvious to the not so clear, including adding value, saving money, sharing resources and expertise, ensuring greater efficiency, improving quality, and avoiding unnecessary duplication. Less obvious benefits that are important and significant to the health and vitality of the colleges, universities, and consortia include the expansion of learning opportunities for students, faculty, and staff; the additional knowledge and

NEW DIRECTIONS FOR HIGHER EDUCATION, no. 120, Winter 2002   © Wiley Periodicals, Inc.

expertise gained when collaboration and cooperation occur; and the synergy that often occurs when a critical mass of like-minded people engage in a common task. Leveraging resources can enhance, expand, and develop the organization's pursuit of mission.

Nevertheless, factors like other pressing campus issues, attitudes, money, and personnel can impede the success of any effort striving to leverage resources. Inexperience with collaboration or distrust of the process might stand in the way of leveraging resources, as would the inability or unwillingness to commit to a plan of action. There may be differing interests or concerns that need to be addressed or a lack of institutional support that becomes a barrier when individual institutional members of a consortium hope to optimize the available resources collaboratively.

In 2001–2002, the more than one hundred members of A Community of Agile Partners in Education (CAPE) explored the issue of sustainable change and its impediments in a series of seminars, "Aligning for Shared Success." Although the seminars concerned successful sustainable change, the same kinds of impediments that occur while seeking sustainable change are also encountered when resources are leveraged.

Because leveraging resources is often a change agent, CAPE's suggestions for sustainable change also apply. To overcome these concerns, CAPE suggests that sustainable change comes from a shared vision: goals must be stated and success defined: Will it be an institutional success, a consortial success, or a collaborative success? Real teamwork is often required for the optimal leveraging of resources. Any resistance to change must be overcome, the stakeholders must be engaged, and a reward system must be in place before resources can be leveraged successfully (A Community of Agile Partners in Education, 2001).

Success in leveraging any kind of resource does not mean that each institution or member must share identical goals. In fact, the goals for leveraging resources can be reached even if those who come together to optimize their resources share only a broad consortial goal, such as saving money; the institutional goals for how much money will be saved, how it will be saved, or how the savings can and will be realized might be vastly different.

An array of resources can be leveraged. Human resources can be leveraged; people with their knowledge and skills are resources that lend themselves well to the leveraging that comes from collaborative activities. Curricular resources can be leveraged; different kinds of joint programs can take on added value in an educational setting. Services and products can be leveraged; a joint human resource office, shared risk management through insurance, or a combined hazardous waste pickup saves money and time.

Ways to Leverage Human Resources

Associated Colleges of the St. Lawrence Valley (ACSLV) is an educational consortium with four members: St. Lawrence University, the State University of New York at Canton, the State University of New York at Potsdam, and

Clarkson University. This is a consortium of two- and four-year colleges and universities and a combination of public and private colleges and universities. Located in northern New York within ten miles of each other and only twenty miles from the Canadian border, their rural location and small enrollment (under ten thousand combined graduate and undergraduate students) mean there is a great need to leverage human resources that offer additional opportunities for faculty, staff, and students. ACSLV endeavors to add value to members through developing ample opportunities to achieve cost savings in the area of human resources.

Human resources at ACSLV are often maximized by bringing together groups of people who share a common interest but do not constitute a critical mass on their own campus or do not have access to funding to offer certain professional development programs. For example, in 2000, a committee of human resource personnel from ACSLV organized an effort to bring in the American Council on Education (ACE) to offer training for faculty in administrative positions. First, a vision of what might be accomplished before, during, and after the workshops was explored, and the possible outcomes were developed and shared before the program went forward. The logistics were planned during many meetings and communications, trust was established among all the players (the members of the planning committee, the academic deans, the participants, and the consortium staff), and program offerings were examined and reviewed before a contract with ACE could be negotiated and signed.

A number of issues needed to be ascertained if the program was to be successful: What were the needs of faculty on each campus who were in administrative positions? Was there support at the highest levels? Who would be included? Would the fee be divided equally or charged by number of participants? Who would be the contact person with ACE and arrange logistics? All of these concerns—vision, goals, financial accountability, and logistics—and others were examined.

About eighty faculty members from four campuses attended this two-day event, which featured modules on roles and responsibilities of department chairs, shaping mission and leading change, creating cultures of quality in academic departments, and conflict management. In this venture that sought to maximize the potential of certain faculty members, the institutional goals for how to increase the faculty members' potential, how the energy of the saved potential would be used, and the rewards or sanctions for the success or failure of the ACE program were very different. These differences in outcomes can and should be articulated and refined during the planning process so that effectiveness can be measured and disappointments avoided. In the end, consortium members came together and realized increased faculty effectiveness, additional networking opportunities, and better use of educational resources even though the goals and levels of satisfaction differed for each member.

Another endeavor that reveals differing goals for participants is the educational program at ACSLV that encourages the human development and potential of employees. Clerical employees of the four institutions can attend seminars designed to increase their job efficiency. Workshops about handling difficult people, effective communication, and time management are offered every semester. The member institutions' goals might be vastly different from those of the individuals involved; for example, the institutions might expect that the employee would become more efficient in his or her job, while the employee is interested in advancement. Therefore, the goals are not the same for everyone. Nevertheless, as long as each group of those participating receives something (added value, some sort of contribution to well-being, or a learning opportunity), these different goals are not exclusive.

Other events that leverage human resources at ACSLV include an annual seminar about retirement that focuses on skills and knowledge that employees need as they begin to think about ending their employment association with the institution. These workshops would not be held by the individual campuses because the number of potential retirees does not warrant this, but by combining and leveraging the resources from four campuses, consortium members can offer an important seminar.

Joint faculty appointments and programs are other ways to leverage the human resources of a consortium. ACSLV has a faculty member with joint appointment with two members of the consortium: this faculty member shares teaching assignments and other duties and is an employee of the consortium, with salary and benefits shared equally between the two members. In this way, two small departments on different campuses can share the expertise of this faculty member while the synergy that results is invaluable.

Five Colleges, Incorporated in central Massachusetts has had joint faculty appointments since 1973. In this way, the member institutions can explore new fields and specialized areas that are not represented on any member campuses. This is also a less expensive way to bring leaders in a particular field to the campuses (Peterson, 2001).

Other consortia also offer different opportunities for leveraging human resources. The Colleges of the Fenway (COF), in conjunction with Suffolk University in Boston, offer a leadership management program that helps nominated participants "to continue meeting goals and facing the challenges and opportunities of the future in higher education" (Colleges of the Fenway, 1999).

Five Colleges also offers a management training program for supervisors. Although the ten workshops held each year were originally grant funded, the consortium, through the schools, has leveraged those resources and now supports the program (Five Colleges, 2002).

Tri-College University (Concordia College, Minnesota State University, and North Dakota State) presents, as do others, a career fair that offers students from those three campuses an opportunity for face-to-face contact and potential interviews with prospective employers (Davis, 2000). This program maximizes the potential of the students as well as increases the opportunities for business and industry.

Ways to Leverage Curricular Resources

Many consortia typically offer cross-registration: students can enroll in courses offered on another campus within the consortium. ACSLV has offered this opportunity to students since the early 1970s and serves many students each academic year in this way. Money does not change hands in this cross-registration exchange, even though there is a disparity between the public and private tuition rates. This exchange of students leverages the curricular resources that are available to students and optimizes the faculty.

There are varied ways that other consortia leverage curricular resources. In a twist on the cross-registration idea, Tri-College University offers a world studies seminar series taught by faulty from each campus, creating an opportunity for students to enroll in courses that are not offered on any of the campuses (Davis, 2000).

Leveraging curricular resources can allow consortia to meet, develop, expand, and actualize an institution's mission. ACSLV is in the preliminary planning stage of determining a way to leverage curricular resources and meet its public service commitment to northern New York. Because of the dearth of secondary school administrators in this region, the consortium has formed the Educational Leadership Academy of Northern New York (ELANNY). One of ELANNY's goals is to provide a master's degree (and to offer a doctorate after the successful launching of the joint master's degree) in educational administration that leverages the graduate curricular resources of three members by combining leadership with educational and business administration.

The University Heights Association (members are Albany College of Pharmacy, Albany Law School, Albany Medical College, and the Sage Colleges of Albany and Troy, all in New York) plans to leverage its curricular resources by offering a master's degree in genetic counseling. Two campuses will provide faculty and courses for the degree, and a third will contribute counselors and a director and host the counselor rotations (Frazer, 2001).

These opportunities for offering degrees that combine elements of several campuses have impediments. None of them is insurmountable, but as Frazer (2001) points out, many of these concerns are pressing: Will the consortium offer a joint degree, or will a particular campus do so? Can existing faculty be used? Will the final offering be accredited? Nevertheless, none of them is likely to hinder the final leverage that can be obtained by this coordination of curricular resources.

Ways to Leverage Products and Services

Shared risk management is an area in which resources can be leveraged: services can be jointly purchased, and the risk involved in those services is shared in ways that save money and adds greater efficiency. COF employs a risk manager who inventories the needs of the members concerning property and liability and then goes out for a bid. The risk manager thinks strategically for the member institutions to ensure that the resulting policy provides coverage that is needed and required. When a flood recently affected members of COF that share this risk manager, they realized significant cost savings because the institutions split the insurance deductible, so each was saved from the full impact of the $50,000 deductible. In addition, a broker employed by COF provides education on risks that might be encountered in higher education settings—experiential learning off-campus, emergency preparedness, and safe driving—so that potential claims will be minimized.

Recruitment advertising for potential employees is another service shared by some COF members. After a marketing study to determine the best medium and location for publicity, members committed to a joint contract that included on-line job services. Saving money, increasing the visibility of the institutions, and avoiding unnecessary duplication were benefits realized by leveraging the services of the advertising agency.

A shared contract negotiated by COF with a temporary employment agency has several important economies of scale. The agency maintains a pool of people who are interested in working in higher education, so temporary needs can easily be met with qualified personnel. Reduced rates are applied to contracts, and there is a reduced cost if the temporary employee is hired into a permanent position. As part of the corporate mission of the temporary agency, any unplaced temporary workers are "loaned" to a nonprofit agency. By virtue of their contract with this agency, COF is able to designate where these "loaned" temporary workers are placed, ensuring positive public relations for themselves in the process (Colleges of the Fenway, 2002).

Student health insurance lends itself to consortial relationships. Most schools have some form of health insurance for students, and it makes sense to negotiate jointly with an agent to achieve the best contract to suit various needs. Five Colleges and COF have offered student health insurance through a common vendor, and the cost savings are substantial (Five Colleges, 2002; Colleges of the Fenway, 2002).

Five Colleges leverages resources by sharing the services of a recycling coordinator who assists the member campuses with education about recycling. Some waste materials are sold, and others are recycled; the individual members continue to be guided by their own campus policies (Five Colleges, 2002). In this instance, it is obvious that when making the best cooperative use of resources and achieving success, a participating institution need not give up anything. Often, it really is a win-win situation.

Conclusion

It is easy to leverage resources, and impediments for the most part can be met and overcome. When only money is involved (as is usually the case with leveraging services and products), the path is straightforward and easy. Finances are, after all, easily measured, and effectiveness is easy to document.

Programs that seek to leverage human and curricular resources are more difficult because the results are more qualitative. The attempts may enter into the area of an institution's mission, increased synergy, or learning opportunities, none of them easily measured.

Just having new ideas is not enough. There must be exploration to see if a new way of leveraging resources can be accomplished and if it is the right idea at the right time for the consortium and its institutions. There must be a team leader who will own the new idea and spend the time and energy to share this concept with others. There must be enthusiasm, and goals and outcomes must be projected. Key persons must be encouraged and supported to buy into the concept of leveraging resources. The commitment to the long term must be present in order to succeed, and success in leveraging resources will follow if these areas are recognized and thoroughly explored.

References

Colleges of the Fenway. *Leadership Management Program.* Boston: Colleges of the Fenway, 1999.

Colleges of the Fenway. *Joint Purchasing Initiatives.* [http://www/colleges-fenway.org/initiativesPurchase.htm]. Jan. 14, 2002.

A Community of Agile Partners in Education, Aligning for Shared Success. Bethlehem, Pa.: A Community of Agile Partners in Education, 2001.

Davis, N. "Upcoming Career Fair Is Unique Chance for Students to Meet Many Employees." *Trice: The Tri-College University Newspaper,* Nov. 2000, p. 4.

Five Colleges, Incorporated. *Programs in Administration.* [http://www.fivecolleges.edu/adminprog.html]. Jan. 14, 2002.

Frazer, C. "University Heights Association Collaboration on a Degree Program." *ACL Newsbrief,* Dec. 2001, p. 2.

Peterson, L. M. ". . . . From the Vantage Point of Three and a Half Decades." In Carol Angus (ed.), *Annual Report 1999–2000.* Amherst, Mass.: Five Colleges, 2001.

ANNEKE J. LARRANCE *is the executive director of the Associated Colleges of the St. Lawrence Valley in Potsdam, New York.*

2

Higher education consortia are forming K–12 partnerships and alliances that are linking with individual public schools and their school systems.

Partnerships with K–12 Education

Rosanne Druckman, Lorna M. Peterson, M. Sue Thrasher

Partnerships between institutions of higher education and public schools have flourished for twenty years. The primary motivation has been the sense of urgency first noted in *A Nation at Risk* (National Commission on Excellence in Education, 1983), which set the stage for sweeping reform and the call for additional resources. With this call for change came new opportunities for partnerships.

In recent years, policymakers and politicians from all levels of government have made education a priority, and the public continues to identify education as a major domestic concern. The national call to fix failing schools has fostered a dynamic and sometimes volatile environment in public schools, particularly in urban areas.

School boards and educators are experimenting more, and often they are eager to reach out to new resources in the community, including local colleges. In turn, institutions of higher education have recognized their responsibility and self-interest in working with their colleagues in the K–12 arena.

This new attention to public education has resulted in a shift away from the traditional partnership model that involved departments or schools of education exclusively. Partnerships today are more inclusive, involving academic departments as well as administrative staff.

Diversity of Partnerships

In states and regions where a consortium of higher education institutions exists, the consortium has often taken a leadership role in developing partnerships with the schools. These partnerships are as diverse as the consortia they represent, each responding to the particular situation and needs of

New Directions for Higher Education, no. 120, Winter 2002 © Wiley Periodicals, Inc.

the local community. Some offer tutoring, others engage in the movement for school reform, many provide access to higher education for students and teachers, and still others offer professional development and community development. The *2000 Consortium Directory* (Association for Consortium Leadership, 2000) lists thirty-two consortia that are involved in some kind of partnership with public schools. These include partnerships from every corner of the nation, in rural and urban areas, local, regional and statewide, private and public, and a combination of both. The Consortium of Universities in the Washington Metropolitan Area provides a compendium of over 370 partnership programs between its member institutions and the public school systems in the areas. (For a full listing, go to Partnerships in Education on the consortium Web site: http://www.consortium.org.) At the other end of the country and in a nonurban environment, the Claremont Colleges in southern California are engaged in a partnership with the Claremont Unified School District "to promote, facilitate and document cooperative programs between The Colleges and The School District." At least two consortia, the Alliance for Higher Education in Texas and the Community of Agile Partners in Pennsylvania, both with sophisticated information technology assets, provide support and expertise in technology and professional development opportunities to teachers and schools through distance learning.

The Hartford Consortium for Higher Education and Five Colleges, Incorporated represent two very different consortia and two very different partnerships. The Hartford Consortium, in Hartford, Connecticut, is an alliance of higher education institutions, public and private, graduate, professional, and two-year, secular and religious, that has served the Greater Hartford community since 1972. (The members of the consortium are Capital Community College, Central Connecticut State University, Hartford Seminary, Rensselaer at Hartford, Saint Joseph College, Trinity College, University of Hartford, and University of Connecticut.) While individual institutional members of the consortium operate over thirty-five programs linked with local public schools, the consortium has focused its efforts on a college-access program. Five Colleges, Incorporated, established in 1965, is in a largely rural area in central Massachusetts with campuses in three towns within a ten-mile radius of each other. Its members are four liberal arts colleges and the flagship campus of a state university. (The members are Amherst College, Hampshire College, Mount Holyoke College, Smith College, and the University of Massachusetts at Amherst.) The Five College Public School Partnership serves all the school districts in the four counties of western Massachusetts. Like the Hartford Consortium, individual institutions link with public school districts in a variety of programs that range from teacher certification graduate programs to informal teaching opportunities. As a consortium, however, the Five College Public School Partnership's primary focus is professional development for teachers.

Hartford and the Hartford Public Schools

In the past ten years, Connecticut has been frequently cited as having the highest per capita income in the country. "Hartford's children, however, are the sixth poorest in the Country compared to their counterparts in cities of 100,000 or more" (The United Way of the Capital Area, 1995). Plagued by decreasing population, low levels of home ownership, and a weak mayoral form of government that discourages accountability, the city of Hartford has experienced significant challenges since the recession of the early 1990s. The city is the largest school district in Connecticut, enrolling 22,538 students, of whom 53.1 percent are Hispanic, 41.4 percent are African American, and 4.7 percent are Caucasian. Appropriately 65 percent of students are eligible for free or reduced-fee lunches at school (Connecticut Department of Education, 1999).

In 1997, many community leaders were concerned about the well-publicized failures of the Hartford Public School system: a board that was often deadlocked, a revolving door of top staff leadership, and student test scores that were consistently the worst in the state. With support from Connecticut's governor, John Rowland, the state passed legislation that brought Hartford schools under the control of a state-appointed board of trustees. Since the trustees were appointed, student achievement, as measured by Connecticut's standardized tests, has improved, and the superintendent hired in 1999 by the trustees has shown leadership and vision in managing the system. There are still enormous challenges, however: the dropout rate remains high, and 83 percent of fourth graders read below state goals (Connecticut Department of Education, 2000).

Career Beginnings. In 1986, Career Beginnings was created as a local site of a national urban education initiative. When the program began, only 37 percent of Hartford's high school students were attending college after high school graduation. The mission of Career Beginnings, "to increase the percentage of urban youth who graduate from high school, pursue higher education and obtain a job with the potential for advancement," has remained constant even after the pilot phase ended and the connection with the national effort was discontinued.

The consortium offers an administrative home to a program that fits well with its goal to develop innovative approaches in addressing educational issues. As an alliance of colleges, the consortium is able to acquaint students with local higher education options as well as opportunities throughout the country. Because Career Beginnings makes a significant contribution to the greater Hartford community and is also a source of local students for member institutions, the board continues to support its linkage to the Hartford Consortium.

Career Beginnings serves approximately 150 high school juniors and seniors each year. Most participants are midrange students, achieving a C− or better academic average. The majority of students are referred by guidance counselors, and some are self-referrals. In addition to twenty workshops on a range of topics related to college admissions, career exploration, and personal development, the program offers students a staff counselor and a volunteer community mentor. Counselors review academic progress and refer students to tutoring or any community service needed. Mentors review application deadlines, take students to college interviews, and encourage them to work hard to meet their goals. Because many of the students are the first in their family to attend college, the guidance offered by the program is particularly valuable.

A Model of Collaboration: Colleges, Public Schools, and Businesses. All of the member institutions of the consortium provide some type of assistance to the program and collaborate on programming. The Hartford Public School system is an important partner because it refers students, consults on an ongoing basis about participants, and offers office space to the staff counselors in the high schools. The business community plays a key role in relationship to the mentoring component. Many of the mentors come from area corporations, with the remainder from nonprofits and civic groups. Area corporations encourage employees to become mentors by sponsoring recruitment events at the companies.

Results. The results for the students who complete the eighteen-month program are impressive, and even stunning. Consistently, over 92 percent graduate from high school and attend college. The program tracks students after their freshman year, and over 90 percent complete the first year of college. There are now over a thousand alumni of the program, and some have returned to be mentors for other students.

Funding. In order to operate the program efficiently, the colleges provide a number of in-kind services, including space, facilitators for workshops, and volunteers. Funds to pay program staff are raised mainly from local corporations and foundations. There have been many consistent supporters in the local funding community because of the high achievement levels of students who complete the program. Because of the in-kind services and the number of volunteers associated with the program, the annual budget is relatively small at $166,000.

Future Challenges. The future challenges revolve around finding resources to reach students earlier in their school career and continuing to operate a program almost entirely on soft money. Fundraising requires a dedicated and time-consuming effort because most of the grants have to be renewed annually. It is difficult to make significant expansions such as reaching out to freshmen at the high schools because of the annual pressure of raising funds for the core program that reaches juniors and seniors.

The Five College Public School Partnership

The Five College Public School Partnership was organized during the 1983–84 academic year with the support of the presidents of the five member institutions, the state Department of Education, and the Massachusetts Teachers

Association. From its inception, the partnership has served all forty-four of the diverse school districts in the four western Massachusetts counties of Hampshire, Hampden, Franklin, and Berkshire. Included in this mix are large urban, suburban, small town, and rural districts.

The mission of the partnership has remained constant: to develop mechanisms for strengthening communication and sharing resources between the schools and the colleges. Its focus is in the discipline areas of the sciences and humanities rather than educational instruction and administration. Program planning is always done collaboratively, and over the years, this has resulted in networks of both college and school faculty who share a common academic interest and excitement about teaching. Indeed, the partnership has been able to thrive and be effective in large part due to the willing participation of respected senior college and school faculty.

Major Program Initiatives. Throughout its history, the Five College School Partnership programs have ranged widely in terms of format, participants, and content. Formats have included two- to three-week summer institutes, one- and two-day conferences, after-school workshop series, special interest forums, day-long sessions during school time, Saturday sessions, and individual summer research fellowships. Participants are primarily classroom teachers, but special sessions have also been organized for administrators. The partnership office serves as a communications and networking center for both school districts and higher education. It publishes a quarterly newsletter for over seven thousand readers and fields requests for information, referrals, and program support from college and school faculty and administrators. (Currently, the partnership is in the process of transferring its newsletter to a Web-based publication and has developed special e-mail alert lists for various disciplines.)

The organization of the partnership coincided with a nationwide concern about mathematics and science education, and the partnership responded by organizing major programs in this area. These included projects funded by the National Science Foundation, Eisenhower funds through the Massachusetts Board of Higher Education, and Partnerships to Advance Learning in Mathematics and Science, the statewide systemic initiative. The focus in all of these projects was to provide teachers with content knowledge that could be translated to the classroom.

In 1997, the partnership helped establish the Science, Technology, Education, and Mathematics Teacher Education Collaborative (STEMTEC), a five-year project funded by the National Science Foundation. The University of Massachusetts is the lead institution in a unique collaborative that includes the four liberal arts colleges of the consortium, three area community colleges, and area school districts. STEMTEC's focus is on improving math and science teaching at the undergraduate level, thus improving the preparation of future teachers and encouraging more students to consider careers in teaching. (The URL for the STEMTEC Web site is http:// k12s.phast.umass.edu/~stemtec.)

Math and science education have been a major component of partnership programs, but concerted effort has also been made to maintain programs in the arts and humanities. "The Native American Experience in New England" series began with a summer institute in 1988 and has continued as an annual program area focused on the history, culture, and ongoing community life of Native Americans in the Northeast. "Witness for Freedom" was a multiyear project that enabled teachers to explore the use of primary source documents in the classroom and eventually yielded a curriculum guide that matched the documents to the Massachusetts social studies frameworks. Currently under discussion is the possibility of developing a partnership between K–12 districts and college faculty to improve the teaching of preservice teachers in the humanities.

Challenges. The partnership faces three major challenges as it seeks to carry its work into the future. The first is the ever-changing nature of educational reform, resulting in a more cautionary approach to professional development on the part of both teachers and administrators. The current climate of educational reform in the state mirrors the national picture in that there are many contested areas: high-stakes tests for students and new teachers, the formula for funding charter schools, and the recruitment and retention of high-quality teachers.

Funding also remains a major challenge. While the long-term commitment of Five Colleges, Incorporated is demonstrated by the inclusion of the partnership as a line item in its annual budget, program funds need to be raised annually, requiring time and energy for program development and collaborative planning. The most likely scenario for the future is that math and science will continue to have a wider funding base of support, and the arts and humanities will have to scrabble and forage.

Finally, the partnership must continue to provide programs that are open to all western Massachusetts teachers, while developing mechanisms for working in a more focused way with specific districts.

Conclusion

College-school partnerships will continue to grow and flourish as both K–12 and college educators respond to the need to ensure that public education remains a healthy arena that can provide quality education for all students. Institutions of higher education have a vested interest in the excellence of K–12 education because they need students who come prepared to do college-level work. Both K–12 and college educators have an interest in recruiting and preparing future teachers. Existing partnerships have done a great deal to close the gap between K–12 and higher education, and consortia are particularly well prepared to support such efforts. A review of the following list of consortium partnerships illustrates the diversity among them:

Associated Colleges of Central Kansas, McPherson, KS, http://www.acck. edu

Associated Colleges of Illinois, Chicago, IL, http://www.acifund.org

Associated Colleges of the St. Lawrence Valley, Potsdam, NY, http://www. associatedcolleges.org

Association of Independent Kentucky Colleges and Universities, Danville, KY, http://www.aikcu.org

Atlanta University Center, Atlanta, GA, http://www.auc.edu/auc.html

Central Illinois Higher Education Consortium, Peoria, IL, http://www. cihec.org

Claremont Colleges, Claremont, CA, http://www.claremont.edu

Colleges of Worcester Consortium, Worcester, MA, http://cowc.org

Committee on Institutional Cooperation, Champaign, IL, http://www. cic.uiuc.edu

Community of Agile Partners in Education, Bethelem, PA, http://www. acape.org

Consortium of Universities of the Washington Metropolitan Area, Washington, D.C., http://www.consortium.org

Council of Independent Colleges in Virginia, Bedford, VA, http://www. cicv.org

Five Colleges, Incorporated, Amherst, MA, http://www.fivecolleges.edu

Hartford Consortium for Higher Education, West Hartford, CT, http:// www.hartnet.org/hche

Higher Education Consortium of Metropolitan St. Louis, St. Louis, MO, http://www.heccstl.com

Hudson Mohawk Association of Colleges and Universities, Latham, NY, http://www.hudsonmohawk.com

Illinois Prairie Higher Education Consortium, Mattoon, IL, http:// www.iphec.org

Lehigh Valley Association of Independent Colleges, Bethelem, PA, http:// www.lvaic.org

Midwestern Higher Education Commission, Minneapolis, MN, http:// www1.umn.edu/mhec

New Hampshire College and University Council, Bedford, NH, http:// www.nhcuc.org

New Orleans Educational Telecommunications Consortium, New Orleans, LA, http://www.gnofn.org/~noetc/wizzc.html

Northeast Ohio Council on Higher Education, Cleveland, OH, http:// www.noche.org

Northwestern Michigan College University Center, Traverse City, MI, http://www.nmc.edu/~ucenter

Pennsylvania Association of Colleges and Universities, Harrisburg, PA, http://www.pacu.org

Professional Arts Consortium, Boston, MA, http://www.proarts.org

Southern Illinois Collegiate Common Market, Herrin, IL, http://www.
siccm.com
Southwest Virginia Public Education Consortium, Richmond, VA, http://
www.vamsc.org
Tri-College University, Fargo, ND, http://www.ndsu.nodak.edu/tricollege
Valley of Virginia Partnership for Education, Harrisonburg, VA, http://www.
jmu.edu/outreach
West Suburban Post-Secondary Consortium, Oak Brook, IL, http://www.
wshec.org

References

Association for Consortium Leadership. *2000 Consortium Directory*. Norfolk, Va.:
Association for Consortium Leadership, 2000.
Connecticut Department of Education. *Connecticut Department of Education Strategic
School Profiles for 1999*. Hartford: Department of Education, 1999.
Connecticut Department of Education. *Connecticut Department of Education School Profile
2000–2001*. Hartford: Department of Education, 2000.
National Commission on Excellence in Education. *A Nation at Risk*. Washington, D.C:
U.S. Government Printing Office, 1983.
The United Way of the Capital Area. *United Way of the Capital Area Regional Snapshot*.
Hartford: The United Way of the Capital Area, 1995.

ROSANNE DRUCKMAN *is executive director of the Hartford Consortium for
Higher Education in West Hartford, Connecticut.*

LORNA M. PETERSON *is executive director of Five Colleges, Incorporated in
Amherst, Massachusetts.*

M. SUE THRASHER *is coordinator of the Five College Public School Partnership
in Amherst, Massachusetts.*

3

Economic development provides an opportunity for higher education institutions to collaborate on public service programs that contribute to national, regional, and community vitality.

Facilitating Economic Development Through Strategic Alliances

John B. Noftsinger, Jr.

A new economy is quickly transforming one of the most staid pillars of the nation. A quiet revolution is occurring on college and university campuses across the United States. The changes extend beyond the land grant model to other smaller research, doctoral, comprehensive, and baccalaureate-granting institutions. However, the impetus for change is the same: responding to a new economy in a world of changing boundaries, global competition, rising expectations, finite resources, exploding technologies, expanding knowledge base, changing societal norms, national security concerns, and an uncertain economy.

Strategic relationships with other institutions of higher learning and sectors of society (K-12 school divisions, private business and industry, other state or federal government agencies, and social service and other nonprofit organizations) are gaining increasing attention as a mechanism for public and private institutions to meet pressing existing needs, take advantage of emerging opportunities with a minimum of resource investment, and deliver cost-effective and innovative public service programs. As pressure from stakeholders, including students, tuition-paying parents, and taxpayers, has increased for institutions to be more efficient with regard to the educational value they provide to students, so have corresponding public expectations for accountability and economic development increased with regard to public service contributions.

The number and complexity of higher education partnerships with external communities has increased in the past twenty years. These linkages represent a tremendous variety of goals and interests and are a reflection of

NEW DIRECTIONS FOR HIGHER EDUCATION, no. 120, Winter 2002 © Wiley Periodicals, Inc.

seismic societal forces. Strategic alliances are a strategy used to address local, regional, state, national, and even international challenges. The proliferation of the partners and goals of the programs underlines the blurring of boundaries in society and the importance ascribed to these ventures by policy- and stakeholders inside and outside the academy. Higher education has the opportunity to become a visible national asset through playing a more tangible role in economic and national security causes through strategic alliances.

Higher Education as a Critical National Infrastructure

Higher education in the United States today is facing increasing pressures from inside and outside the academy to restructure and reform in order to meet the needs of society better with a minimum of new resource investment. Some observers suggest that this pressure is the natural progression of the education reform movement that began with efforts to revitalize basic education in the 1980s. Others contend that the efforts to reshape American higher education are the results of a skeptical public that believes that during the past two decades, higher education in general has become increasingly isolated from the mainstream of American life and exceedingly expensive.

Trends toward a closer relationship with the needs of society have ebbed and flowed throughout the past one hundred years of the modern American university. The land grant efforts to revitalize agriculture, basic education initiatives, and science research to counter *Sputnik* are all examples of commendable responses to societal challenges. But today the response is different and includes all types of institutions. It is driven by a technological revolution and a national security challenge on a scale never experienced before. The challenge of workforce development in an economy fueled by human talent as its major raw material underlines the opportunity.

A Critical Infrastructure. In June 2001, the Executive Office of the President, Office of Science and Technology Policy, and National Science Foundation sponsored a White House conference entitled "A Workshop on Critical Infrastructure: Needs in Interdisciplinary Research and Graduate Training." The workshop examined the contributions that higher education should be making to protect critical national infrastructures. According to the proceedings of the workshop, leaders in higher education should recognize and creatively respond to the opportunities and realities that the national critical infrastructure challenge provides. In order to do this effectively, it is paramount that the academy embrace a vision that balances basic and applied research, interdisciplinary program deployment, and engagement through strategic alliances. If the challenge of the national security is taken seriously and appropriately and creatively responded to, higher education itself can be viewed as more vital to the important challenges of the nation because of its direct impact through research, education, and service.

The recommendations of the workshop are bolstered by the stunning events of September 11, 2001.

Convergence in Education. Comparisons between higher education and the telecommunications industry offer the most vivid picture of what may be in store for American higher education. Technological developments, competition, and alliances are driving macro- and microsystemic changes. The competition and blurring of education and training from private companies in the area of higher education and training illustrate educational convergence. The movement to output-based competency standards away from input-indexed seat time as a metric of higher education productivity measurement will continue as certificate programs and private providers compete with traditional baccalaureate and master's degrees for entry into lucrative jobs. The bundling of educational services and one-stop shopping will become the norm in higher education as it has in telecommunications. The competition for a higher education institution may well be American Online Time Warner instead of the traditional college competitor down the road. This convergence underlines the importance and opportunity for strategic alliances for survival.

Strategic Alliances in the Academy. As Godbey (1993) predicted, powerful forces have converged within American society and have forced colleges and universities to cooperate and share resources at unprecedented levels. These forces present both dangers and opportunities. Competition through cooperation can be a strategic tool to maintain institutional distinctiveness and enhance competitiveness.

A common practice in American higher education since the turn of the century is gaining significant attention in corporate America as an innovative method of delivering products and services at minimum cost and maximum profit. Since the first Claremont Colleges were founded in 1925, and perhaps even before, colleges and universities have been working together in creative ways through consortia and partnerships to maximize resources and meet programming needs that they could not do in isolation. Private industry and business have recently adapted this concept for their own purposes by forming joint ventures for a specific purpose.

Godbey (1993) first examined the opportunity to reinvigorate higher education consortia and partnerships as a result of the agility and strategic alliance movement in business and industry. He elaborates, "And yet, the argument for virtual organizations may be simply an updated version of the argument for postsecondary consortia" (p. 39). Activities such as K–12 outreach, continuing education, economic development, and distance learning are prime environments in which to implement strategic alliances in higher education.

Economic Development and Higher Education

Society has looked to higher education to solve business-related problems and serve as a vehicle for economic development tracing back to the beginnings of land grant universities, agricultural extension, and the applied work of research universities. The current environment of dramatic changes and societal expectations places a new emphasis on the potential for higher education to contribute to economic development in new and better ways. The opportunity is highlighted by the nature of the change in the world. The search for better cooperative relationships between business and postsecondary educational institutions has become a dominant theme in contemporary university management (Matkin, 1990). The recession of 2002 and the events of September 11, 2001, have nudged government officials to rethink the role of academic research in enhancing technological innovation, national security, and business development. Legislators and policymakers demand economic benefits from university research and from the collection of organizational and human talent and resources located at these institutions and supported through public funding. Private institutions too view their own viability and prestige as linked with their local communities, underlining the opportunity for public-private alliances (Matkin, 1990).

The traditional missions of research, teaching, and service are being reshaped to respond, and what has emerged is a new paradigm of the entrepreneurial university. This new model is more directly involved in the commercialization of research and embraces technology in all aspects of teaching, research, and service. Institutions are more vigorously engaged in regional economic development, use a more market- and quality-driven approach to curriculum development, and are more concerned about management efficiencies. As a result, the university's goals and ways to measure those goals are being dramatically redefined and expanded (Smilor, Deitrich, and Gibson, 1993).

Economic development activities range from minor technical assistance to small businesses to complex relationships that attempt to develop new technologies, the applications of which have not yet been conceived in many instances. Much of the current economic development activity of the academy focuses on bringing higher and K–12 education, business and industry, and local, state, and federal government together in new and creative ways in order to compete for business expansion and attraction nationally and internationally. The Association of Governing Boards (2001) identifies economic development activity as one of ten public policy issues for higher education.

Not everyone has welcomed the increased emphasis on economic development in the academy. Faculty members, private citizens, and public watch groups have criticized the close relationships between business and higher education as dangerous developments because they blur lines and jeopardize higher education's traditional role of objective and detached critic. Others cite the potential for conflict of interest, diminished open exchange of ideas as a result of the protection of intellectual property, and the potential for technology transfer and commercialization to diminish the role of basic research and the opportunity to discover new knowledge as points of tension.

A Framework for Engagement

As a result of internal and external forces, higher education institutions are increasingly examining opportunities to form relationships and enhance community service functions for a variety of compelling reasons.

In a recent extensive study of higher education economic development activity in Virginia, Noftsinger (1997) found an extremely entrepreneurial and innovative array of public service strategic alliances. Information from the study yielded a public service framework that demonstrates proactive and entrepreneurial engagement on the part of the academy that may serve as a useful template to future program development:

- Strategic, systemic, and collaborative initiatives
- Enhanced access to resources and technology assistance
- Targeted industry initiatives
- Organizational development and enhancement
- Research, development, and policy analysis
- Human resource development
- Reciprocal agreements and technology transfer

The first three program types demonstrate an academy that is much more proactively engaged with external constituents. The last four represent a more traditional, if not appropriately responsive, role for the academy. The framework may be especially useful from a public policy perspective for planning the outreach activities of the academy.

Programmatic Examples of Economic Development Alliances

Based on the framework provided, an example of each program type from the Valley of Virginia Partnership for Education (VVPE) will be highlighted. The VVPE is an outreach program of James Madison University's Research and Program Innovation in the office of the Vice President for Academic Affairs and has either played a role in facilitating or has engaged in a strategic alliance with the programs highlighted here.

The VVPE is a strategic, systemic, and collaborative endeavor that has been a catalyst for a variety of programmatic reforms. An intersector partnership founded by the education and business communities of the Shenandoah Valley in October 1991, it serves as a regional resource center, program source, and coordinating group to encourage and support partnerships among education, business and industry, and government entities that seek to improve educational quality, resource accessibility, educational access, economic development, and workforce preparation for the greater Shenandoah Valley region of Virginia. The VVPE seeks to maximize the educational investments of participating communities through partnerships, resource sharing, coordinating of activities, joint projects, and enhanced communication. The subsequent programs illustrate this philosophy.

Basic School Eastern Consortia. The Basic School Eastern Consortia is a network center hosted by Research and Program Innovation at James Madison University (JMU) and is an example of a strategic, systemic, and collaborative initiative. Inspired by the challenge that the renowned scholar and former president of the Carnegie Foundation for the Advancement of Teaching, Ernest Boyer, issued for campuses to engage in the scholarship of engagement, the Eastern Consortia assists schools in creating learning communities of excellence based on Boyer's four priorities (1995): the School as Community, a Curriculum with Coherence, a Climate for Learning, and a Commitment to Character.

Shenandoah Valley Partnership. The Shenandoah Valley Partnership (SVP) seeks to facilitate economic development in the Shenandoah Valley area and is another example of a strategic, systemic, and collaborative initiative. This regional partnership encompasses the cities of Buena Vista, Harrisonburg, Lexington, Staunton, and Waynesboro along with the counties of Augusta, Bath, Highland, Rockbridge, and Rockingham. The partnership currently has a board of directors that represents the public and private sectors. The colleges and universities in the region actively participate, and the program is hosted by JMU's Research and Program Innovation and administered as a sponsored program. The partnership, which serves a regional population of just over a quarter-million throughout an area of approximately thirty-five hundred square miles, focuses on marketing the region and strategic enhancement. The SVP administers state funds for competitive regional economic development projects that include a heating, ventilation, and cooling target sector study and training center, regional technology council formation, and the Work Keys center at Blue Ridge Community College that endeavors to close gaps between workers' skill levels and workplace skill demands through a national workplace skills analysis system.

Rural Revitalization—JMU/Page County/Town of Shenandoah Partnership. The VVPE and the Office of Economic Development and Partnership Program, units of JMU Research and Program Innovation, launched a strategic, systemic, and collaborative initiative with an economically challenged neighboring county in 1997. In a focused attempt to support economic revitalization efforts, the university extended its resources through a partnership with Page County and the Town of Shenandoah. The region had been adversely affected by railroad and manufacturing job losses and was experiencing higher unemployment than the surrounding area. In order to develop and implement the plan, the university provided a graduate student funded by the county government and supervised by Research and Program Innovation. The successful development and implementation of the plan prompted the county to employ the student on graduation as director of economic development.

Building on the success of the county, the Town of Shenandoah, located in Page County, requested that JMU assist it in a similar manner. A graduate assistant funded by the town and under the supervision of the university designed a revitalization and marketing plan for the town. A key component of the project was the revitalization of a sixty-six-acre former industrial tract of land owned by the town. Environmental concerns regarding the property brought together a collaborative partnership that resulted in the receipt of a $200,000 brownfields redevelopment grant from the Environmental Protection Agency. The town was the smallest jurisdiction in the country to receive such a grant, which was to determine whether the site was contaminated from previous industrial use and if the property could be remedied for future use. The alliance was expanded to include the University of Virginia School of Architecture, which used the brownfields intervention as an applied learning experience for academic work. The intervention ultimately resulted in grants and technical assistance of just under $1 million for the redevelopment of the town. In addition to being a successful economic development initiative for the town, the opportunity for graduate students to have hands-on experience in public administration and architecture proved invaluable to the employability of the students. Two JMU graduate students have since been employed full time by the town to manage the projects and have moved onto important government positions with the state and federal governments. Moreover, the town has become confident in its ability to build alliances and call on the assistance of regional higher education partners.

Shenandoah Valley Technology Council. The Shenandoah Valley Technology Council (SVTC), established in 1997 through a grant written by the office of Research and Program Innovation at JMU, is an example of improving access to resources and technology assistance. The council membership consists of business, government, and education leaders acting as technology design, infrastructure, and application advocates and users. The council focuses on serving the greater Shenandoah Valley. The SVTC promotes, encourages, and enhances technology-based business development as a complement to the valley's natural resources through a variety of content-based programs and career networking programs. A program example is the Valley E-Business Forum, a series of programs that help small businesses use e-commerce applications.

Virginia Technology Alliance. The ten regional technology councils in Virginia comprise the Virginia Technology Alliance (VTA), which was formed in 1998. The VTA is an example of a targeted industry initiative. JMU, Virginia Tech, the University of Virginia, and Old Dominion University have worked with business, industry, and government leaders to create the alliance. The mission is to encourage and support the growth and recruitment of businesses and other organizations throughout Virginia that develop, produce, and use technology and facilitate the establishment of new technology companies and organizations. It supports the efforts of the regional technology councils in promoting Virginia's technology economy, advocates for issues important to the growth and development of innovative technologies and technology-based organizations in the commonwealth, educates state and local policymakers by providing a representative and objective source of information and counsel on technology issues, and communicates the economic importance of technology to Virginia's education, civic, and business leaders.

Virginia's A. L. Philpott Manufacturing Extension Partnership. This partnership seeks to foster economic growth by enhancing the competitiveness of Virginia's small and medium-sized manufacturers and is an example of an organizational development and enhancement alliance. The regional partnership office for the Shenandoah Valley is located on the JMU campus and is hosted by Research and Program Innovation. The program provides affordable, high-quality assistance to help companies increase productivity, lower costs, identify growth opportunities, improve technology application, and strengthen their leadership team. The partnership is a network affiliate of the National Institute of Standards and Technology Manufacturing Extension Partnership, a national network of more than seventy manufacturing extension partnership centers that have helped thousands of manufacturers over the past decade. Resources include private consultants, community colleges, universities, and government agencies.

Virginia's Manufacturing Innovation Center. Working as a close ally of the Philpott Manufacturing Extension Partnership, Virginia's Manufacturing Innovation Center (VMIC) focuses on building the capacity of small to medium manufacturers in Virginia. The project is another example of an organizational development and enhancement alliance and is hosted as a sponsored program at JMU and the Center for Innovative Technology. Blue Ridge, Dabney Lancaster, and Piedmont Virginia Community Colleges are all active partners, along with the Virginia Tech and Virginia Commonwealth University engineering programs. The mission of VMIC is to hone the competitiveness of Virginia's smaller manufacturers and help them build a strong economic foundation through a well-trained workforce, accessible advanced information technology, and modern production management techniques.

William R. Nelson Institute for Public Affairs. The William R. Nelson Institute, another program inaugurated by JMU Research and Program Innovation, is an example of a research, development, and policy analysis alliance. With research and policy agreements with Johns Hopkins University, George Mason University, the Romanian American University, the Technical Institute of Moldova, and Moscow State University, the institute is dedicated to the study of political violence and global terrorism and to the development of educational programs in Eastern Europe to facilitate economic development and global understanding. The institute was created after considering world situations and concerns within the context of the post–cold war era. It employs the skills and resources of the university in addressing these problems as an important element of enhanced prospects for stability. A number of the institute's open-source, nonclassified studies have been sponsored by the U.S. government as a result of the increased interest of stability in Eastern Europe and western and central Asia.

Workforce Improvement Network. A partnership of JMU, the Virginia Literacy Foundation, the Virginia Community College System, and the Virginia Department of Education, the Workforce Improvement Network (WIN) is a human resource development partnership. Founded in conjunction with the VVPE in 1996, WIN encourages and supports the development and expansion of customized, foundational basic skill instruction for Virginia's workforce. This network of program developers provides assistance to employers seeking to improve their employees' education within the context of the workplace. Foundational basic skills include reading, writing, math, problem solving, interpersonal communications, critical thinking, English as a Second Language, and the general equivalency diploma.

Commonwealth Information Security Center. The mission of the Commonwealth Information Security Center (CISC), a reciprocal agreement and technology transfer alliance, is to support Virginia as a leading provider and beneficiary of information security services, policies, and products through research, education, technology transfer, and practice. The program was founded in 2001 as a strategic alliance among JMU, Virginia Tech, George Mason University, and Hampton University. It is funded by a $4.1 million competitive grant from the Commonwealth of Virginia and has matching support from business and industry that brings the total scope of the project to almost $10 million over four years. It is housed at JMU as an interdisciplinary center of the College of Integrated Science and Technology and the Department of Computer Science. One of the major events for CISC is a national conference that teams it with the VVPE, the VTA, the SVTC, and the JMU Office of Research and Program Innovation to focus on the national security concerns of information and cybersecurity and to build information security as a key economic sector for the regional and state economy.

Partnerships Are the Key: Making Peace with the Neighboring Valley

Boyer (1994) described a "New American College" that places a distinct emphasis on public service partnerships to meet the needs of society and solve problems. He described it as an institution that celebrates teaching and selectively supports research, while also taking special pride in its capacity to connect thought to action and theory to practice. It should organize cross-disciplinary institutes around pressing social issues. Undergraduates should participate in field projects, relating ideas to real life. Classrooms and laboratories would be extended to include health clinics, youth centers, schools, and government offices. Faculty members should build partnerships with practitioners who come on campus as lecturers and student advisers. Effective strategic alliances hold the key to this transformation.

From the beginning of recorded human civilization, human beings have often regarded the inhabitants of the next valley as savages and those persons residing in their own valley as mostly intelligent, noble, and civilized. Therefore, it stands to reason that the process of entering into strategic alliances with different, suspicious, and sometimes competing valleys of society is not without its perils. However, it could be argued that remaining in one's own valley and concentrating on building defenses to keep those savages from across the mountain out may prove to be even a more perilous venture than engaging in collaboration.

Conversely and somewhat contradictorily, human beings, often from the same valley, have also exhibited the tendency to bind together in times of peril. The events of September 11, 2001, and the ensuing war on terrorism and natural disaster responses provide vivid evidence. Higher education strategic alliances to support economic development provide a unique opportunity to serve local, regional, state, and national interests through connecting teaching, research, and service capacities to its stakeholders at an important juncture in the history of the nation.

References

Association of Governing Boards. *Top Ten Policy Issues for Higher Education in 2001–2002.* Washington, D.C.: Association of Governing Boards, 2001.

Boyer, E. L. "Creating the New American College." *Chronicle of Higher Education,* Mar. 9, 1994.

Boyer, E. L. *The Basic School: A Community for Learning.* Princeton, N.J.: Carnegie Foundation, 1995.

Godbey, G. "Beyond TQM: Competition and Cooperation Create the Agile Institution." *Educational Record,* Spring 1993, pp. 37–42.

Matkin, G. W. *Technology Transfer and the University.* New York: Macmillan 1990.

Noftsinger, J. B. *Public Service Partnerships and Higher Education Restructuring in the Commonwealth of Virginia.* Ann Arbor, Mich.: Bell and Howell Information and Learning Company, 1997.

Smilor, R. W., Deitrich, G. B., and Gibson, D. V. *The Entrepreneurial University: The Role of Higher Education in the United States in Technology Commercialization and Economic Development.* New York: UNESCO, 1993.

JOHN B. NOFTSINGER, JR. *is associate vice president of academic affairs for research and program innovation and executive director of the Valley of Virginia Partnership for Education at James Madison University in Harrisonburg, Virginia, president of the Shenandoah Valley Technology Council, and vice president of the Association for Consortium Leadership.*

4

Community development initiatives offer special opportunities for partnerships among institutions of higher education.

Consortia and Institutional Partnerships for Community Development

Mitchell R. Williams

The need for effective community development to address social, economic, and environmental issues is perhaps stronger now than at any other time. Making communities functional and livable is critically important to our society. There is a renewed interest in using the resources of higher education to assist communities and regions through community development initiatives (Livermore and Midgley, 1998; Usnick, Shove, and Gissy, 1997). To illustrate the contribution of colleges and universities to building sustainable communities, this chapter examines the development of community leaders through institutional partnerships and consortia involving different types of institutions of higher education.

Contemporary community development has come to represent the idea of improving communities through diverse and inclusive participation of citizens, and it is associated with the advancement of strong leadership. Leadership development programs train citizens to work together to effect positive change, and they exist in dozens of communities across the country. These programs help men and women learn how to perform roles that are essential to successful community development, and they are often offered by community-based organizations.

There is a fundamental dilemma associated with many community leadership development programs. Although most of these programs emphasize the importance of collaborative leadership, the sponsorship of these programs themselves all too often does not involve any institutions of higher education or just a single institution in collaboration with nonacademic organizations. In order to make comprehensive community leadership development programs as effective as possible, multiple institutions of higher education should work collaboratively—with each other and with community-based organizations—to plan, implement, and evaluate these programs. For practitioners interested in community development, collaboration among diverse institutions of higher education provides opportunities to address community challenges by bringing together different philosophies, points of view, and curriculum resources.

Higher Education's Role in Community Development

Higher education's place in community development has changed and evolved, with a role that varies from "activist participants to dispassionate analysts" (Baird, 2001, p. 122). Usually reacting but sometimes initiating community change, colleges and universities have been shaped by and helped to shape the communities that surround them. Although Hamilton (1992) referred to community development as "a stepchild of the educational establishment" (p. xiv), these institutions have become increasingly willing to serve as active partners in community development activities (Usnick, Shove, and Gissy, 1997). Higher education is now considered a driving force for citizen participation and is positioned to become a major component in community development strategies. Service is one of the three basic missions of higher education, and community development activities are now incorporated into the mission of many institutions of higher education.

One of the best ways for colleges and universities to demonstrate their commitment to community service is through participation in the sponsorship of community leadership development programs. Successful leaders often seek to build coalitions and sustain cooperative participation. Developing leaders who can meet the demands of this century will require new mind-sets and methodologies within these programs. For example, Rost (1993) pointed out the need to develop people who want to engage in leadership as collaborators: "people who want to work collaboratively with other people to change organizations, committees, and or society, who want to work in teams to institute change that reflects the majority of the team members" (pp. 101–102).

It is clear that collaboration should play a significant role not only in the curriculum of community leadership development programs but also in the sponsorship of these programs. Different organizations naturally bring different strengths to these programs, and the right combination of sponsoring organizations can mean the difference between a successful program and a disappointing one. Too often, however, program sponsorship either excludes institutions of higher education or does not take advantage of the benefits of involving multiple institutions acting in a partnership or consortium. A consortium or institutional partnership has a broader perspective, more extensive linkages in the community, and more diverse resources than any single institution. A community leadership development program created through efforts involving a consortium or partnership of institutions of higher education should have tremendous integrity, value, and ingenuity.

One obstacle to the involvement of higher education in community leadership development programs may be a perception that community organizations do not want colleges and universities to share in program sponsorship. Data indicate that this is not the case. A study was conducted to determine what constitutes ideal partnerships in the sponsorship of community leadership development programs and where the disparities are found when comparing current sponsoring partners and the perceived ideal partners (Williams and Wade, forthcoming). Sixty-seven randomly selected administrators of community leadership development programs responded to questions about current collaboration in the sponsorship of their programs and about the organizations they perceived to be ideal partners in such efforts. The organizations reported as currently involved in the sponsorship of community leadership programs were then compared with organizations perceived as ideal partners for sponsoring these programs. The largest difference between the current partnerships and the ideal partnerships was found among three types of institutions of higher education: public four-year universities, private four-year colleges and universities, and community colleges. Forty-three respondents indicated that public universities would be included in an ideal partnership for collaborative relationships in sponsoring such a program, but only sixteen respondents indicated public universities were already involved in the sponsorship of their programs; similarly, thirty-one respondents felt community colleges would be involved in ideal partnerships, but only twenty-one had two-year colleges among their current program sponsors.

The involvement of institutions of higher education in program sponsorship is far below the level practitioners desire. The results of the study suggest that institutions of higher education should be more open to participation in community leadership programs and that the participation of multiple institutions of higher education, acting in partnership, may be especially valuable to these programs. Also, in a period of public scrutiny and accountability for institutions of higher education, colleges and universities should be eager to work with community organizations in order to demonstrate leadership and service.

Leadership Jackson: A University–Community College Partnership

Western Carolina University is a public, regional, comprehensive university located in a rural valley between the Blue Ridge and Great Smoky mountains, fifty miles west of Asheville, North Carolina. Its service area includes some of the most rural counties in the state, in a region that historically lags behind the rest of North Carolina in terms of per capita income, employment opportunities, and educational attainment. Western has conducted several community development outreach programs with services for small business owners, local government officials, and managers of nonprofit agencies. In 1997, a group of citizens in Jackson County, the university's home county, met with university leaders to discuss the need for a leadership development program to prepare promising leaders to help address the community's historical and emerging challenges. The university was quick to respond to this request and placed administrative responsibility for the new community leadership development program in its Division of Advancement and External Affairs.

With limited human and financial resources, it was evident from the beginning of the process that a collaborative effort would be needed to initiate and sustain the program. The first task of the committee formed within the university was to identify community-based organizations that might be interested in partnering with it to design, plan, and implement a community leadership development program. The first call was to the local community college.

Southwestern Community College (SCC) is a comprehensive two-year institution serving Jackson and two other counties in southwestern North Carolina. Although the institutions are separated by little more than five miles in a rural county, there had been little collaboration between SCC and Western on community development initiatives. Nevertheless, SCC quickly became the first and most important partner in the leadership program planning process. As veteran community college leaders themselves, SCC's president and administrative staff had a great deal more experience than their university colleagues in community education, including adult and noncredit continuing education, along with numerous other services to county residents. Based on studies of the social, economic, and political environment within Jackson County, they helped to identify other community stakeholders to include in the program planning process (for example, the chamber of commerce, major employers, and the county planning office) and helped to build a coalition of support for a community leadership development initiative.

The university–community college partnership worked extremely well in planning, designing, and implementing what was called the Leadership Jackson program. Program leaders at both Western and SCC realized that institutional diversity and differences in institutional mission are great strengths of the higher educational system and in higher education's response to community needs. For example, large public research universities and community colleges have different but equally important missions and diverse but valuable roles in responding to external community demands for services such as community leadership development. Western and SCC, institutions with very different missions, recognized and appreciated this diversity when they collaborated with each other to establish a community leadership development program. Each institution could bring its unique strengths to focus on the leadership program. For example, the university could serve as a source of knowledge and information, provide data on trends and issues related to community leadership development, supply expertise, and (if necessary) conduct applied research related to community concerns identified through the leadership program.

Community colleges emphasize community service and have developed processes to position themselves to play major roles in resolving community issues such as leadership development. In addition to a tradition of community service, the community college could contribute to this community development project through in-depth knowledge of the community and the ability to customize programs. By combing the strengths of their institutional missions as well as pooling resources, the university and community college provided a community leadership development program that was much stronger and more comprehensive than the program either institution would have offered on its own.

By publicizing their successful joint effort regarding Leadership Jackson, Western and SCC enhanced their images in the community and on their campuses as well. Community leaders are now more likely to see these institutions as resources for community development rather than as simply major employers in the community. The successful collaboration of these two institutions in community leadership development was followed by other cooperative initiatives that benefited the community and surrounding region.

On each campus, one successful partnership has led to others. Through faculty-led initiatives, these neighboring schools have subsequently worked more closely on professional development projects and enhanced academic articulation agreements.

Considerations for Success for Community Development

By forming strategic alliances, colleges and universities from different sectors of the higher education community can take community development to new levels. The Leadership Jackson project discovered discrete best practices for community development activities involving institutions of higher education in consortia or institutional partnerships:

• It is vital for four-year institutions to use cooperative and collaborative relationships with community colleges to promote community development. Institutions must determine an appropriate division of labor and avoid duplication or competition within the partnership (see Ferro, 1993).

• The participation of community colleges is helpful in identifying community or regional needs that can be addressed through consortial initiatives.

- Participation in the partnership or consortium should increase each institution's capability to respond to community development needs.
- It is important to publicize collaborative activities and achievements in university publications in order to communicate to the campus community the importance of becoming involved in community development partnerships.
- Colleges and universities are often "well-kept secrets in their service areas. The buildings are visible, but community leaders don't see much there to which they can relate" (Ferro, 1993, p. 25). Consortia and partnerships involving different types of institutions of higher education can help to surmount these challenges by giving service to the community a high priority and by making new as well as existing services more readily available and accessible to the community.
- Consortia and institutional partnerships can facilitate efforts to recognize and reward the community development activities of faculty and staff. Although the publish-or-perish mind-set will likely continue on individual campuses, cooperative efforts may help to convince leaders in higher education to uphold the pool of valuable expertise and resources available to community development and provide rewards to faculty for university-based community initiatives.
- Pooling resources from two or more campuses can produce community development programs that cannot be initiated by one campus alone, but there must be a clear commitment on the part of institutional leaders, including an assurance of financial and human resources, if community development partnerships are to be effective.

Barriers to Success

In addition to factors that might contribute to the success of higher education alliances related to community development, the Leadership Jackson case study identified several potential obstacles to successful interinstitutional collaboration. First, turf issues play a role in many institutional relationships in higher education. During the initial planning of Leadership Jackson, there was a tendency among some at SCC to resist the participation of Western Carolina University in what was seen as a community education function. Conversely, there were those at the university who felt the community college tried to be "all things to all people" whenever an education-related need was identified in the community. Strong leadership and constructive dialogue among staff members put an end to this obstacle.

Another barrier that was quickly overcome might be referred to as academic snobbery, or the idea that a community college should not be an equal partner with a regional comprehensive university in a community development project. A few people at the university questioned why SCC was considered an equal partner in Leadership Jackson when Western was clearly the "senior" (that is, more prestigious) institution. Any hint of academic snobbery was set aside when it was agreed that the university chancellor and the community college president would have equal roles in the opening ceremony of the leadership program and in presenting certificates at the end of the program.

Finally, institutional self-centeredness can be a barrier to collaboration. All institutions within the higher education community have strengths, and diversity of mission is a strong point of the higher education system. Collaborating partners must acknowledge and celebrate their institutional differences rather than minimize or deny them; there should also be an acknowledgment that the partnership needs the expertise offered by each participating institution. For Leadership Jackson, institutional self-centeredness was quickly dispelled when staff members at the two institutions emphasized the areas where the roles of community colleges and universities could complement each other rather than lead to competition.

Conclusion

Community leadership development should be a collaborative function that develops community leaders through partnerships involving multiple institutions of higher education. The process offers an ideal opportunity to demonstrate the potential of multi-institutional collaboration and partnership among diverse institutions of higher education. For example, interinstitutional relationships involving two- and four-year institutions of higher education can be especially effective in community development and may be more beneficial to the participating institutions than had previously been considered (Pennington and Williams, 2001). Particular benefits can result from encouraging institutions to experiment with nontraditional institutional partnerships (for example, involving community colleges and four-year liberal arts colleges or community colleges and research universities) in providing community services such as leadership development.

Community college leaders may be more likely than leaders of four-year institutions to consider participating in interinstitutional agreements to provide community service such as leadership development. This is probably due to the fact that community service is a central part of the mission of the community college. Two-year colleges seem more capable of forming the essential associations critical to addressing specific community concerns.

Higher education can make a unique contribution to community development initiatives. Partnerships and consortia involving diverse colleges and universities can be especially useful in these efforts. The synergy created by bringing together diverse institutions of higher education through consortia, institutional partnerships, or informal alliances can create community development opportunities that no single institution could possibly provide. Moreover, nontraditional institutional partnerships like community colleges and research universities can be especially effective in providing essential services such as community leadership development.

References

Baird, L. L. "Higher Education's Social Role: Introduction to a Special JHE Issue." *Journal of Higher Education,* 2001, *72*(2), 121–123.

Ferro, T. R. *Improving the Quality of Continuing Higher Educators' Leadership Role in Economic and Community Development Planning.* Indiana, Pa.: Indiana University of Pennsylvania, 1993. (ED 361 511)

Hamilton, E. *Adult Education for Community Development.* Westport, Conn.: Greenwood Press, 1992.

Livermore, M., and Midgley, J. "The Contribution of Universities to Building Sustainable Communities: The Community University Partnership." In M. D. Hoff (ed.), *Sustainable Community Development: Studies in Economic, Environmental, and Cultural Revitalization.* Boca Raton, Fla.: Lewis, 1998.

Pennington, K., and Williams, M. R. "A Primer for Community College Consortium Building." *Academic Leadership,* 2001, *8*(2), 3–5.

Rost, J. "Leadership Development in the New Millennium." *Journal of Leadership Studies,* 1993, *1*(1), 91–110.

Usnick, R., Shove, C., and Gissy, F. "Maximizing Community Development Through Collaboration." In J. P. Pappas (ed.), *The University's Role in Economic Development: From Research to Outreach.* San Francisco: Jossey-Bass, 1997.

Williams, M. R., and Wade, V. *Collaboration in Community Leadership Development Programs: What Constitutes an Ideal Partnership?* Forthcoming.

MITCHELL R. WILLIAMS *is director of leadership programs at the University of North Carolina Asheville in Asheville.*

5

Leveraging higher education resources to build a state's workforce takes dedicated commitments from business, education, and public policy leaders. Consortia can play an important role as facilitator and convener.

Leveraging Higher Education for Workforce Development

Thomas R. Horgan

Higher education's strategic role in developing a workforce is a topic of intense interest and vigorous debate both within the academy and throughout the wider community. Various stakeholders—students, parents, business leaders, elected officials, K–12 educators, higher education faculty members, administrators, trustees, and others—are all influencing factors in the emerging direction that higher education is taking in the complex realm of workforce development, skills training, and higher learning. As this confluence of diverse pressures and market demands bears down on the postsecondary sector, institutions are responding in creative new ways. They are providing new degree programs that are in high demand, and new partnerships and alliances with businesses, local high schools, and even other colleges are being formed to deliver specific and timely training. It is indeed proper that as postsecondary institutions attempt to meet their obligations in workforce development that consortia be included; they are a unique resource, convener, and safe forum for discussion and possible collaborative action.

Attention to workforce development strategies is having a direct impact on higher education institutions as they reexamine their role and mission. Clearly, this examination is heightened as states competitively maneuver for leadership in economic growth and industrial development and look to higher education institutions as a leveraging resource. Meeting the pressures of diverse demands from their various stakeholders while simultaneously maintaining a faithful commitment to higher education's core mission and principles is a daunting and conflicting, if not nearly impossible, task. This chapter examines postsecondary responses to workforce development in New Hampshire with the hope that the lessons learned and achievements identified will serve a significantly broader audience.

Building New Responses to Workforce Demands

New Hampshire colleges and universities are striving to meet the growing demand for highly skilled knowledge workers, while simultaneously reaffirming a commitment to developing an educated and responsible citizenry. Educating students beyond the simple delivery of content material is a point of keen debate far from being settled on or off campuses. However, it is a debate that seems to be garnering the interest of an ever wider array of stakeholders. This argument is indeed fueled by many factors, including the aggressive growth and increasing competition of proprietary institutions, the perception that the cost of traditional higher education is spiraling out of control, and vocal expressions from students who are demanding a monetary return for their educational investments.

Proprietary Institutions. Proprietary, for-profit, higher education institutions have coexisted with traditional public and private nonprofit colleges in New Hampshire for over a hundred years. However, recent aggressive growth in the proprietary arena has caught the attention of the more traditional postsecondary institutions. In New Hampshire, two formerly family-owned proprietary institutions have been sold in recent years to out-of-state corporate interests. Kaplan and the Career Education Corporation (CEC) have each brought a new assertive sense of competition and corporate mentality not previously present in the state. Compounding this concern are changes occurring throughout the region relative to proprietary growth, including the recent location of a University of Phoenix Education Center in Massachusetts. Subtle concerns over the changing landscape have brought heightened unease to the traditional campuses, resulting in a more competitive spirit and concern for survival. Within the consortium, this concern was heightened by the announcement that Notre Dame College in Manchester, New Hampshire, would close in May 2002 as a result of low enrollments and rising expenses

Tuition Costs. The cost of attending college has consistently outpaced inflation over the past decades, and a growing reluctance of students and families to assume overwhelming debt is reaching up to even the middle class. A recently released report from the Lumina Foundation for Education, *Unequal Opportunity* (Kipp, Price, and Wohlford, 2002), points out dramatic disparities in college access caused by affordability indexes, especially for low- to moderate-income students. With a national projected growth rate of high school students of more than 10 percent over the next decade, a corresponding growth in college applications is also anticipated. Many of these students will be high-need and minority students for whom costs will be an overarching concern. New Hampshire statistics indicate that 74 percent of the state's public and private institutions are unaffordable for dependent low-income students. Although some of the data in this national report have been questioned for accuracy and implications, its warnings are unquestionably disconcerting and a concern for colleges that are enrollment and tuition driven.

The Postsecondary Education Opportunity (Mortenson, 2000) reports that the national average cost of attending a public two-year college is over $7,000 annually and that public four-year college costs are averaging over $11,000. In New Hampshire, with the highest community college tuition in the country and the second highest four-year public college rates, these numbers are even higher and raise serious concerns over accessibility and flexibility.

Monetary Return. Assessing the economic benefits of a college education in this environment is understandably of growing interest. Certainly, the benefits of a college education are measurable in a multitude of ways, but anticipated increases in the personal income of the college educated attracts the most attention from students, parents, and the general public.

The Postsecondary Education Opportunity (Mortenson, 2000) reports that for families headed by persons with a bachelor's degree, the anticipated lifetime income will be about $1.6 million more than the anticipated income of families headed by persons with only a high school diploma. Speculation that there is a connection between increased postsecondary enrollments and anticipated increases in lifetime earnings is not new, but is perhaps more dominant now than at any other time in the history of postsecondary education. As attendance in higher education increases, there is a growing public perception that higher education is a right to which every citizen is entitled. What is less certain is how institutions will be constituted in the future to ensure equal access to higher learning as a prerequisite to participating in the economy.

New Hampshire serves as a distinct example of the connection between educational attainment and income levels. Ranked the fifth highest state in percentage of the population with a bachelor's degree or higher and sixth highest in per capita income, New Hampshire demographics point to a strong connection between educational attainment and income levels.

Investing in Futures

Given the relationship between income and education, it is difficult to explain some of the other statistical rankings for New Hampshire, especially relative to its high educational achievement levels and its low direct state investment in education. State expenditures on higher education in New Hampshire consistently rank last among the fifty states in state financial support, forty-seventh in state scholarship support, and only at the national average for high school students going on to postsecondary education. About 69 percent of New Hampshire high school graduates go directly from high school to college, a surprisingly low number given the high percentage of adult residents who hold baccalaureate degrees. Also disturbing for those concerned about building the state's base of knowledge workers is the fact that New Hampshire students who pursue higher education reportedly leave the state at the alarming rate of 51 percent to attend college compared to a national average of 18 percent.

Higher Education Summit

A consistent question raised among many higher education administrators in New Hampshire is how a state that ranks so strong in personal income levels and educational attainment can rank so low in these other important indicators. In an effort to address this issue, a higher education summit was convened in 1999 by a number of organizations concerned with the state's higher education sector. From this statewide gathering, some enlightening answers began to emerge.

This summit, "Creating Knowledge Workers for the New Millenium," brought together more than one hundred leaders from state government, industry, the public policy arena, and public and private postsecondary education institutions to focus on the trends, challenges, and opportunities facing New Hampshire in meeting its future needs for an educated workforce. Released at the summit was a research report, *The Status Report on Higher Education in New Hampshire* (Gittell, 1999), commissioned collaboratively by the New Hampshire Higher Education Assistance Foundation, the New Hampshire College and University Council, the New Hampshire Postsecondary Education Commission, and the New Hampshire Charitable Foundation.

Report Findings. As the business leaders, elected officials, and educators learned, virtually all companies in the state were having difficulty filling skilled positions and pointed to this trend as the most important economic concern threatening the state's role in high-tech employment leadership. At this time, New Hampshire enjoyed the distinction of having the highest percentage of high-tech workers in the country, but what was not widely recognized was how many of these workers had come from other states. This report revealed that the state ranked first in the Northeast and eighth in the nation with respect to in-migration of residents. Surprisingly, it was reported that more than 80 percent of New Hampshire's household heads holding a bachelor's or advanced degree are not native to the state, nor did they likely attend college within the state. Therefore, the report indicated, the affinity that many residents have for their state's higher education institutions is not a part of the state's ingrained culture. Obviously, the fact that New Hampshire is small (geographically and in population) influenced these trends, as does the fact that so many higher education institutions are located within a short drive of New Hampshire's borders.

The summit report highlighted that for the state to continue to meet the need for skilled workers, it would have to do a much better job in educating its own citizens. Projecting that the growth rate of college graduates in New Hampshire would have to double or even triple to satisfy the rising demand for skilled labor captured the attention of the summit participants. Noting that "brainpower is the horse power of the knowledge economy" (p. 3), the research report also projected that the state could face a crippling drought in the next century as competition with other states for educated knowledge workers grows.

Summit Recommendations. The summit report offered possible ways that New Hampshire might react to these workforce and higher education trends, suggesting three primary recommendations: increasing higher education aid and grants to state residents based on both need and merit, giving more help to institutions so they can reduce tuition, and eliminating the New Hampshire state statutes allowing local municipalities to impose property taxes on nonprofit educational property (dining halls and dormitories). The report also warned decisions makers, "There are already indications that inadequate investment in higher education is slowing New Hampshire's economic growth" (p. 13). Reflecting on these findings, summit participants agreed to regather within six months with a plan for building an organizational bridge among the state's business leaders, educators, and elected officials with a commitment to creating a world-class education system to produce a world-class workforce.

Speaking in response to the summit findings and recommendations at a follow-up press conference on March 14, 2000, the president of the New Hampshire Business and Industry Association called for a conversation among the states business leaders, higher education trustees, and administrators on the topic of higher education's response to new markets, the future of distance learning, and the linkage between business needs and higher education's role in the new economy. He went on to express an expectation that "a new wave of cooperation will change the way we do business." These and other similarly reported comments from the state's business leaders were well received within the higher education community and confirmed that the summit had generated a wider base of interest in the topic of higher education and its importance to the workforce.

Institutional Responses to New Ways of Doing Business

Higher education institutions in New Hampshire have responded to the changing demands of the state's economy for skilled workers in a multitude of ways, both subtle and substantial. Directly in response to the summit's report documenting the need for more high-tech workers in the state, many institutions announced new program offerings in high-tech and high-skilled areas (Seufert, 2000). Daniel Webster College, a small, private, four-year college in Nashua with a national reputation in aviation aeronautics, announced in January 2000 that it was establishing a committee of regional leaders in computer science and education to expand and enhance its computer science program and cited the summit report findings in its press release. Identifying the state's high dependence for bringing in out-of-state knowledge workers, the college announced a new software development degree program. In announcing the program, the college stated its belief that "one long-term solution to the growing need for skilled knowledge workers is the expansion of high-quality, scientifically based undergraduate and graduate programs in computer science which are both rigorous and practical. This new addition to the curriculum is designed to allow students to comprehend software properties and management of the software development process" (p. 1).

At Southern New Hampshire University in Manchester, the emphasis is on developing a traditional residential campus along with quality distance-education programs. Largely known for its business offerings, the university was among the first in the nation to adopt Blackboard software as a standard for on-line educational delivery, require an asynchronous format to allow students in different time zones and schedules to interact in the same class, and pioneer in providing the entire suite of campus services completely on-line. With eight thousand on-line enrollments in 2002, the program is the largest in the state, offering an Internet-based approach to higher education and delivering educational opportunities to both traditional and nontraditional students. In January 2002, the university received federal funding to construct the first congressionally funded Distance Education Center of Excellence in the nation. This facility will primarily be a research and collaboration center tasked to support the New England region. The New Hampshire College and University Council hopes to work collaboratively with the university as it reaches out to offer support to other consortium members in sharing resources and exploring unique cooperative opportunities in distance learning.

Workforce development is a key component of the mission of New Hampshire Community Technical College System. The system is active in a number of widely recognized workforce development programs. One notable education program, Project Lead the Way, initiates high school students into engineering and engineering technology fields within their high school settings. Again citing warnings from the state's business community and others that New Hampshire has relied too long on the in-migration of technology talent from other states to fuel the economy, the system has dedicated itself to "growing our own" through programs like Project Lead the Way and has brokered new articulation agreements with the University System of New Hampshire, announcing a seamless transfer of credits from the community and technical colleges to university system baccalaureate degree programs.

Consortial Roles

In developing collaboration in and around workforce development in New Hampshire, the consortium has served more as a facilitator and less as a direct catalyst for change. However, serving as a resource, building awareness and interest in the status of initiatives, and bringing attention and understanding to the concerns of the consortium's member institutions have proven instrumental.

Attempting to move institutions simultaneously is no easy task, and the consortium can assert itself only when its presence is desired, welcomed, and viewed as mutually beneficial. When the New Hampshire College and University Council attempted to direct member institutions into a collaborative joint contract for Blackboard services, it became apparent at meetings held among the information technology directors from individual campuses that collaborative intentions were quickly being overrun by on-campus timing issues, budget functions, and individual priorities. Since first exploring this possibility nearly two years ago, today almost all member institutions of the consortium are Blackboard clients. They migrated there separately and independently, yet each cites the consortium's role in facilitating the discussion and employing the possibilities as an influence in their decision process.

Trying to overcome the hurdles of interinstitutional cooperation on the topic of workforce development has proven to be a daunting task. The lesson learned is clearly that the consortium must find how best to serve its members and to accept that it will not always be the cornerstone of new collaborative initiatives, but may simply be the catalyst that drives new endeavors.

Building the Workforce: The State's Role

In July 2000, the federal Workforce Investment Act (WIA) of 1998 was enacted to prepare America's workforce for the new economy and went into effect throughout the country. In New Hampshire, Governor Jeanne Shaheen opted to establish one Workforce Opportunity Council (WOC) as a statewide Workforce Investment Board. In most states, regional WOCs were established to implement the act, but a single-entity approach was chosen in New Hampshire due to the size of the state and as a way to leverage resources most effectively. The WOC board was charged with constructing a world-class, business-driven workforce development system. The council consists of forty-three members, with the majority representing the state's private sector. The rest of the board members represent K–12 education, higher education, and other nonprofit entities. The consortium has participated actively in this statewide effort since its inception.

The WOC's long-range goal is to increase the quality and size of New Hampshire's labor force by investing in programs that increase the education, employment, retention, and earnings of the state's workers and its young people. Major initiatives undertaken by the council include the implementation of a statewide one-stop delivery system that provides access to employment, training, and employment support resources in one location. These New Hampshire WORKS Centers replaced the old state unemployment offices and are designed to assist a broad array of career searches, including those with high skills and degrees. Early indications are that the centers are having some success in changing negative perceptions of state unemployment offices. However, in the light of the good economy of the past few years, changing this negative perception has been a challenge. Now, with the weaker economy, interest in these centers for identifying career opportunities and new pathways to employment may improve. The community technical colleges in the state have also collocated at the centers to assist in identifying training opportunities for applicants. Still in the early stages of development, the New Hampshire One Stop Consortium was awarded the Seamless Service Delivery Award from the U.S. Department of Labor–New England region in 2001 in recognition of providing service excellence.

Since 1998, 69 percent of the WOC dollars in New Hampshire have been used to provide customized training funds for companies to conduct training for individuals and to fund incumbent training for employer consortiums in high-demand occupational areas, including health care, high tech manufacturing, optical electronics, machine and precision manufacturing, child care, and computer applications. The Community Technical College System has provided most of this training. An additional federal grant has been used for technical skills to assist New Hampshire companies in providing individuals with training in the high-tech and precision manufacturing industry sectors. Some of these funds have been used for scholarships to low-income students at two- and four-year postsecondary institutions.

In a separate report commissioned by the WOC on the state's workforce, the recommendation was made that the state develop "a training and education system that is available, affordable, easily accessible, and agile, adapting to market conditions and worker needs" (Gottlob and Gittell, 2001, p. 10). The report went on to recommend that workforce development be focused on areas and groups where the need is highest and the returns the greatest, as "one size" does not fit all. A system of partnerships was recommended with ties to networks of business and community organizations, training providers, and educational institutions to be developed.

The Governor's Youth Council, a working subgroup of the WOC, focuses on ways to link and expand a host of educational reform and youth development programs as part of an overall workforce strategy. The vision of the Youth Council is that all youth will have the knowledge and skills they need to compete in the marketplace of ideas, will reach their full potential, will succeed as productive workers and citizens, and will achieve economic self-sufficiency. Relying on workforce and economic development research indicating that New Hampshire must increase the number of high school graduates and increase postsecondary enrollments and graduation levels, the Youth Council set two goals to structure its work and guide implementation of WIA youth services: to increase the number of young people completing high school and to increase the number of young people going into postsecondary education or skilled employment. Federal funds have been used to implement programs like Jobs for New Hampshire Youth within high schools and on college campuses. These programs, targeted at serving at-risk youth who are in danger of dropping out of school, have had tremendous success in motivating young people to stay in school and progress on to higher education.

Developing a New Statewide Response

In the fall of 2000, the Higher Education Summit participants regathered to consider the recommendations of the working group. The main recommendation generated by the original summit participants was to build an ongoing partnership of the state's business, education, public policy, and nonprofit sectors. In response, the concept to link, integrate, and leverage higher education as a resource for building and securing the state's position as a high-tech employment center and as a quality location in which to live and work was revealed. Guiding principles of access, awareness, and public policy were outlined for the summit participants to assist in determining the purpose and direction of this proposed new alliance:

Access. To ensure access to higher education in New Hampshire for all citizens of the state, including making college more affordable, making transfer credits from one institution to another possible and practical, and helping high school graduates of all ages pursue lifelong learning

Awareness. To strengthen the image of New Hampshire higher education institutions as dynamic, successful settings for educating the state's citizens and providing ongoing training for its workforce

Public policy. To endeavor to enhance the realization of decision makers and the public that important matters require adequate research and thoughtful attention paid to data, as well as ongoing investment in the human infrastructure of the state

Building a Forum

The summit participants proposed that the New Hampshire Forum on Higher Education be founded with a mission to develop and sustain a New Hampshire workforce of highly educated and well-trained knowledge workers. Through a series of follow-up work sessions and focus groups, it was determined that the forum should become an independent entity comprising three equal groups of representatives from business, education, and public policy and that this group would function as the governing body. The New Hampshire Forum is a new state consortium, modeled after a similar organization in North Carolina that focuses on K–12 education and is structured to provide a common table for higher education, K–12 education, business, and public policy leaders to research, evaluate, and address some of the most important workforce development issues in the state and strate-gize on how best to leverage postsecondary education to build and sustain the state's leadership in high-tech and high-skill employment opportunities.

The forum has put together a board of fifty-one members, has selected a full-time executive director, has secured funding for two years of opera-tions, and has begun the process of building a strategic plan and consistent message. It provides the basis for important cultural and strategic shifts rel-ative to how New Hampshire's workforce is developed and enhanced.

Conclusion

In order for a state, its higher education institutions, and its businesses to develop a workforce collaboratively that is both responsive and agile, a high level of interest, leadership, commitment, and investment from each sector is required. No single response to this important issue will likely succeed or meet the diverse needs of the various interest groups. In New Hampshire, the building and sustaining of the state's workforce in the past has been driven by a multitude of reactions and strategies in response to both local concerns and federal mandates. Simultaneously, businesses increasingly have been calling for greater coordination of training opportunities and institutional responses to market demands. However, a strategic statewide response has never before been attempted in New Hampshire that focuses on the topic of workforce development in conjunction with the role of higher education. The New Hampshire Forum on Higher Education is the first entity to attempt a statewide strategic response. The level of success that it achieves will be determined largely by the level of consistent com-mitment and investment from the state's public policymakers, business lead-ers, and higher education administrators. If it succeeds, New Hampshire should see dramatic changes in the approach each sector brings to this important topic of workforce development and serve as a model to other states.

References

Gottlob, B., and Gittell, R. *Meeting the Challenge: Higher Education in the New Economy in New Hampshire.* Concord, N.H.: Workforce Opportunity Council, Feb. 2001.

Gittell, R. *The Status Report on Higher Education in New Hampshire.* Concord, N.H.: Workforce Opportunity Council, 1999.

Kipp, S. M., Price, D. V., and Wohlford, J. K. *Unequal Opportunity.* Indianapolis, Ind.: Lumina Foundation for Education, Jan. 2002, *10*(3).

Mortenson, T. G. *The Postsecondary Education Opportunity,* No. 101. Oskaloosa, Iowa: Center for the Study of Opportunity in Higher Education, Nov. 2000.

Seufert, D. *Daniel Webster College Press Release.* Nashua, N.H.: Daniel Webster College, Feb. 2000.

THOMAS R. HORGAN is executive director of the New Hampshire College and University Council in Bedford.

6

Faculty-technology partnerships can be a valuable method by which faculty from different institutions and disciplines share their expertise to enhance teaching and learning.

Technology Partnerships for Faculty: Case Studies and Lesson Learned

Wayne Anderson, Suzanne Bonefas

From its inception in 1991, the Associated Colleges of the South (ACS) has focused on expanding opportunities for faculty in an effort to increase faculty research opportunities and pedagogical skills that would enable them to provide an increasingly challenging and rigorous educational experience for students on the sixteen member campuses. Producing the finest possible educational experience for students underlies the mission of all member institutions.

In the early days of ACS, attention focused on faculty development workshops, with faculty given unique opportunities to learn new approaches to teaching from their peers. Not surprisingly, technology soon became a focus for faculty involved in these workshops. Early adopters wanted to learn more sophisticated ways of using technology and were eager to encourage a second wave of faculty to begin integrating technology into their teaching and research. Key players at this time were determined to demonstrate to their peers how technology could help faculty explore new roles as mentors, coaches, and academic partners in this information age.

ACS presidents, chief academic and fiscal officers, and faculty saw a clear role for the consortium in promoting the use of the technology on the campuses. By working together, member institutions could tap the resources of over two thousand faculty and over four thousand staff members while achieving administrative efficiencies and effecting cost savings in the process.

With funding from the Andrew W. Mellon Foundation, the consortium in 1994 invited faculty to propose collaborative efforts in using technology in new ways—efforts that were both disciplinary and interdisciplinary in nature. The response to that call was extensive, and soon the staff had a myriad of cooperative proposals and plans. From that small beginning emerged nine pilot technology programs, numerous workshops, the creation of a technology center at Southwestern University to serve all the member institutions, and, most recent, the designation of ACS as one of the three component centers of the new National Institute for Technology and Liberal Education (NITLE) funded by the Andrew W. Mellon Foundation.

Case Studies in Technology Partnership

During this period of growth and expansion, the ACS fostered numerous technology partnerships.

Workshops. ACS's Technology Program has offered more than thirty technology workshops for member faculty and staff. From 1995 to 1999, workshops were held on member campuses, with local faculty and staff handling planning and logistics as well as instruction. In spring of 1999, ACS established a consortial technology center at Southwestern University, located in Georgetown, Texas, in order to centralize and streamline the organizational aspects of ACS technology training. The ACS Technology Center, funded by a generous grant from the Andrew W. Mellon Foundation, now serves as a hub for consortial technology initiatives and the site for most ACS technology workshops.

In the early years, workshops included basic introductions to the use of the Internet for teaching and learning, use of productivity software such as word processors and spreadsheets, and beginning-level instruction on Web page creation, focusing on such topics as converting existing course documents to HTML format. After about two years, many individual institutions began offering such basic training to faculty, and users naturally became more proficient with basic technology. This trend has enabled the consortium to offer intermediate and advanced instruction in such topics as multimedia development and large-scale Web site creation and management. Thus, the role of the consortium in technology training has moved toward providing training in more advanced or newer technologies, in which there is not yet enough interest on each campus to support local training. This allows it to be able to achieve the critical mass necessary to justify training on the more advanced levels and to continue to keep a close watch on local offerings in order to continue to fill the gaps in available opportunities for ACS members. Moreover, ACS believes that as more instructional technology professionals begin to be hired by member colleges and meet more needs on the home campuses, the consortium will find itself in a position to draw on their expertise and provide increasingly advanced training and services.

Circuit Rider Program. The goal of the Circuit Rider Program is to provide a mechanism for distributing technology expertise across the consortium in order for all members to benefit. The original plan was for an institution with a technology need (for faculty or staff training, workshops, or consultations) to contact ACS for a recommendation of a staff or faculty member on another ACS campus. Although some circuit rides are initiated in this manner, in practice many of these events have their origins in connections made during ACS technology workshops, seminars, symposia, or other meetings, when individuals realize that they might benefit from one another's expertise. ACS provides an incentive for the "rider" (usually an honorarium) and shares the expenses for the circuit rider with the host campus.

Since its inception in 1997, there have been more than thirty circuit rider events—for example:

- Presentations on technology use from a faculty member made to a department or faculty as a whole
- Workshops on a campus for a department or group (for example, advising a biology department on computerizing a new lab)
- Consultations among ACS information technology (IT) departments (for example, consulting on smart classrooms or help desk operations)

The flexibility of this program has made it one of the most popular services offered by the ACS Technology Program. As with the workshops, the consortium has observed an evolution of how this program is used, with a movement toward sharing more sophisticated skills among faculty and an increasing use among the IT departments to share solutions to similar challenges.

Pilot Programs. In addition to one-time training workshops, ACS instituted a number of pilot programs intended to provide disciplinary or interdisciplinary groups with a longer-term (usually two-year) opportunity for collaboration. Pilot groups have included faculty in archaeology, chemistry, classics, computer science, economics, and modern languages, as well as broader-based groups that explored the pedagogical aspects of technology use and interinstitutional collaborative teaching.

Most of these pilots took the form of an initial summer meeting, follow-up during the academic year (on-line or in the context of professional meetings), and a follow-up workshop the next summer. Faculty from these groups continue to work together, both formally and informally, and several of these projects have evolved into longer-term collaborations. Here is a brief summary of some of these pilots.

Discipline-Based Pilots. The three original pilot programs were discipline based: in chemistry, classics, and economics. The ACS chemists met in the summers of 1996 and 1997 at the University of Richmond. Leaders Raymond Dominey and Emma Goldman introduced participants to software developed and used at the University of Richmond (providing copies to all workshop participants). Invited leaders in the use of technology in the chemistry classroom addressed such issues as mechanisms for engaging the interest of students enrolled in courses for nonmajors. In addition to the summer workshops, ACS chemists have participated in ongoing discussions and have created lasting peer-support connections.

ACS economists also began meeting in 1996, under the leadership of David Anderson of Centre College. Their focus was on digital resources for teaching undergraduate economics. They formed three task forces charged with creating and gathering teaching materials, which completed their tasks using e-mail discussion lists. (These lists were among the first to be created at ACS. Since then, nearly one hundred lists have been created for a variety of ACS constituencies.) The PowerPoint presentations created by ACS economists for introductory economics courses and linked to the group's Web site remain among the most popular downloads on the ACS Web site. The economists presented on the results of their pilot program at the Southern Economics Association in Atlanta in November 1997.

Interdisciplinary Pilots. ACS has sponsored several interdisciplinary pilots, including "Technology and Course Design in the Arts and Humanities," led by Susan Hagen of Birmingham-Southern College. This pilot brought together ACS faculty members in humanities and fine arts to assess the design of their courses in the light of recent technological advances and to consider interinstitutional collaborations. The pilot focused on early modern and eighteenth-century studies, fields that already enjoy a rich tradition of interdisciplinary study. Goals of the group included introducing participants to advanced uses of instructional technology, as well as generally increasing faculty awareness of technology resources in the arts and humanities.

Another pilot program, "Teaching and Learning via the Internet: Development of Team-Taught Interdisciplinary On-Line Courses," led by George Newtown of Centenary College, focused on the exploration of interinstitutional team teaching. Participants developed two courses, each of which was offered at two or more ACS institutions with opportunities for interinstitutional collaboration built into each course. "The Vietnam Experience" was designed and taught by faculty in history, English, international studies, and political science. Students participated in an on-line team-based interinstitutional simulation of the escalation of the Vietnam War. The other course, "Medium and Message: Reading Culture Through Art and Artifact," featured a weekend trip to Poverty Point, Louisiana, where students from two institutions met one another while engaging with material relevant to the course.

Ongoing Collaborations. A number of ongoing collaborations have enhanced ACS's effort to help faculty.

An early pilot program in classics led by Kenny Morrell of Rhodes College and a related pilot program in archaeology led by Mark Garrison of Trinity University have become a longer-term effort to build a digital infrastructure that will support a wide range of collaborative efforts among ACS classics programs. By creating a virtual department of classics, faculty hope to afford ACS students access to the best instruction and scholarly resources in the world without compromising the supportive environment students enjoy at a small liberal arts institution. Components of these programs include interinstitutional courses, summer seminars for faculty development and interinstitutional course planning, and faculty and undergraduate research opportunities in an excavation project in Turkey.

An interinstitutional archaeology practicum, followed by a summer field school at the excavation site, was offered in spring 2002 for the fourth time. This course enrolls students from eight colleges and is team-taught by faculty from eleven colleges. No single ACS institution has the resources to offer a course or research project with the scope of this archaeology program. Because there is more demand for student slots than can be accommodated, the consortium is exploring expansion possibilities. ACS has also offered three interinstitutional courses in intermediate and advanced Latin and Greek, with plans to offer a Latin and Greek course each fall.

Many member institutions are unable to offer a full curriculum in classics beyond the beginning levels. Moreover, because of their need to offer mostly beginning-level courses, faculty in small programs rarely have the opportunity to teach in their area of research specialization. They are afforded this opportunity by the collaborative initiative.

Music. A newer virtual department initiative began when ACS music faculty met at a workshop on technology in the music curriculum held at the ACS Technology Center in 1999. They immediately recognized the promise of technology for collaboration and began to create a number of interinstitutional programs, including jointly led travel-study programs, Webcasting of recitals, and an archive of digital teaching modules. Composition faculty have been particularly interested in ways to share and perform new music and have created the on-line Composition Forum, where faculty and student composers upload recordings and scores of their works in order to share them with colleagues. The forum also includes a mechanism for matching composers with available performers and an ACS composition competition for students. Music faculty are also interested in interinstitutional teaching, taking as their model the successes of the classics program. Indeed, ACS is now exploring the creation of a consortial infrastructure for the creation and delivery of interinstitutional courses in order to provide the opportunity for faculty across the consortium to team-teach across institutions.

Lessons Learned

The consortium has learned many lessons in the process of developing and overseeing technology partnerships, some from successes and some from programs that did not fully meet ACS objectives.

- Programs that have been successful are those that emerged out of strong faculty interest. Faculty suggested ideas based on their real needs and on the opportunities that they hoped to create for themselves and their colleagues. Strong faculty leadership is critical to the success of the programs.

• Technology partnerships can be both disciplinary and interdisciplinary. Many successes have been disciplinary, building on the long-term connections that faculty have with their disciplinary colleagues. In many interdisciplinary areas, however, traditions are less formidable and interests are less entrenched, providing more openness to new efforts drawing on technology. For example, in Latin American studies as well as the emerging area of digital technology and culture, there is considerable receptivity to what might be done in a cooperative fashion.

• Leadership drawn from within the ACS is sufficient to enable the consortium to meet the goals identified. From the start, ACS has been able to identify faculty at member institutions who could envision new programs, organize and lead workshops, create on-line courses, and collaborate in various other ways. These individuals have become more influential and effective each year, building and learning from their ACS experiences.

• It is necessary to be sensitive to the availability of faculty time for these technology partnerships. The efforts can be extremely intensive, requiring more effort and commitment than originally anticipated. Consequently, the possibility of release time should be given considerable attention, and summer planning and curriculum development sessions (with compensation for participating faculty) are critical.

• Incentives for faculty—recognition or release time or a stipend for participating in or leading a workshop or running a pilot program—are essential to produce and sustain faculty participation.

• Ongoing and concurrent evaluations can be particularly effective in guiding or readjusting the technology partnership efforts. A comprehensive report at the end of one of these initiatives has considerable value, and it is essential to conduct such an evaluation. But there should also be an ongoing evaluation, which provides information for any midcourse corrections that might be necessary, particularly when using technology. Students enrolled in interinstitutional courses often provide useful and practical suggestions for adjustments to the technology employed for collaboration.

• Internal and external evaluations of these projects should be undertaken. All ACS project coordinators are asked to conduct ongoing program evaluation, making internal evaluations relatively automatic. The coordinators of consortium programs are held fully accountable for their efforts. At the same time, external evaluators are engaged to provide a fresh and broad perspective on the activity being analyzed.

• It is extremely helpful to be alert to what other institutions are doing in terms of technology partnerships. There is considerable benefit in learning from others—from what they do well and what they do poorly. Studying the efforts of other educational consortia, informal groups of colleges and universities, and important national groups like Educause can be instructive.

- Considerable potential for technology cooperation may exist in challenged or threatened academic departments, particularly those with limited faculty and students. Classics is a good example of this situation. Small departments on each campus mean that faculty have few peers close at hand with whom to share information and collaborate in shaping new approaches to courses and the teaching and learning process. Together, in ACS, thirty classics faculty bring together their considerable resources.

- It is very difficult to find anything too advanced technologically for faculty participants. They seem constantly ready to attempt something new and challenging. Consequently, ACS does not shrink from launching ambitious pioneering efforts in using technology and forge new partnerships.

- It is crucial not to underestimate the progress that can occur from a technology training session or workshop, even one only a few days in duration. Many good ideas can be triggered by formal and informal conversations surrounding a workshop. For example, at an ACS workshop on pedagogy, music faculty convened and exchanged ideas about cooperative possibilities in music, extending to the possibility of a virtual joint department. These possibilities are now rapidly becoming realities.

- The availability of venture capital or seed money is critical. Through its initial funding from the Andrew W. Mellon Foundation, ACS was able to bring together faculty with considerable interest and expertise in technology and encourage them to focus on possible joint ventures. The consortium program was able to capture their attention in a way that would not have been even remotely possible without funding and also without the imprimatur of a major national foundation. Initial funding also enabled the consortium to test some early methodological hypotheses and experiment with pilot programs. That experience enabled faculty technology leaders to identify the areas with the greatest promise for ongoing collaboration.

- It can be very helpful to identify potential projects that can be spun off separately to stand on their own. For example, by extracting classics and archaeology from a broad array of academic areas, ACS enabled these areas to receive the full attention they merited and providing separate and substantial funding has enabled them to leap forward.

Conclusion

As the technology partnerships of ACS have expanded, faculty have reported being able to adopt new roles as mentors, coaches, and academic partners with students in the learning process. In response, students have shared their enthusiasm for new and challenging assignments that are preparing them for the world beyond graduation. The ACS is determined to keep this momentum going and welcomes the opportunity to share experiences and to collaborate with others in making these partnerships even more effective in the future.

WAYNE ANDERSON is the president of the Associated Colleges of the South in Atlanta.

SUZANNE BONEFAS is the director of technology programs of the Associated Colleges of the South.

7

Consortia can develop, support, and sustain long-term interinstitutional faculty collaboration through a variety of structural models.

Creating Networks Through Interinstitutional Faculty Collaboration

Sarah R. Marino

Along with a long-standing focus on administering undergraduate off-campus programs, the Associated Colleges of the Midwest (ACM), a consortium of fourteen private liberal arts colleges, has also been committed to supporting interinstitutional faculty collaboration and development. ACM has traditionally offered faculty the opportunity to network within the consortium; frequently, these networking projects have relied on ACM funds, yet on occasion, ACM has received external funds from a variety of sources. During the past few years, ACM has developed three new opportunities for faculty development and collaboration. ACM received a grant, in partnership with Great Lakes College Association (GLCA) and Associated Colleges of the South (ACS), to fund the Global Partners Project, an initiative fostering collaboration to strengthen international study for undergraduates. It has also received grant funding for two other programs: one focused on developing information literacy and the other directed toward establishing academic collaboration across the colleges. As an external yet familiar agent to the colleges, ACM has used a number of collaborative models to develop and formalize networks supporting faculty collaboration. In the process of working on these grants, the consortium has become more involved in the activities of the ACM colleges, strengthened its representation on campuses, and learned to appreciate the value of flexibility and adaptability.

In addition to these three projects, ACM has, for over twenty years, partially funded two to three faculty workshops annually; other than providing funds, ACM has limited involvement with the workshop and the resulting collaboration. Since 1983, ACM has sponsored a yearly conference with a keynote speaker and several sessions. For each of these events, the ACM academic deans have identified an issue based on their knowledge of faculty needs and interests, and the consortium office has convened a planning committee of faculty and administrators for consultation on a conference schedule and speakers.

Like all other successful consortia, ACM seeks to provide opportunities for faculty members based on existing interests and applicability to the campuses' cultures. ACM relies on the deans of the colleges of the consortium to designate appropriate topics for faculty development. The deans vote to approve the faculty workshops, and they provide institutional funds for at least one faculty member to travel to the conference, so they are engaged both intellectually and monetarily. With the larger conferences, the deans, in consultation with faculty members and other administrators, consider appropriate topics that relate to current issues. Although ACM regularly negotiates the tension between the collaborative instinct and institutional autonomy, the ACM colleges share at least five central attributes: a liberal learning focus, residential campuses, strong academic majors, a range of cocurricular activities, and international interest. Despite their individual campus cultures, the deans consider these shared attributes the basis of their discussion and are able to come to a consensus about conference topics; in doing so, they represent the faculty members, staff, and other administrators. When ACM receives external funding for academic collaboration, however, the funding agent alters the nature of the conversation and extends the consortial network. In these situations, people from outside ACM colleges help shape the faculty development projects by providing funds, structure, and anticipated outcomes.

The three initiatives outlined here are funded by the Andrew W. Mellon Foundation, which has historically supported faculty development projects with international issues, technological expertise, and bibliographic resources. In recent years, the foundation has become even more interested in fostering collaborative efforts. These three faculty development projects build on the relationships and collaborative models that ACM has developed in the past; they also illustrate some of the practical issues that emerge when a consortium gets involved with interinstitutional faculty collaboration.

Global Partners Project

The Global Partners Project was initially funded by Mellon for a three-year period in 1999 and recently received funding for another three years of activities, so the grant activities are at an advanced and well-established stage. ACM has the benefit of having a long-standing relationship with GLCA, sharing several off-campus programs. In addition, ACM and GLCA worked together, aided by grant funds, on the Program for Inter-Institutional Cooperation in Area Studies in conjunction with the International Centers at the University of Michigan. ACS has interests and a structure similar to those of ACM and GLCA. The three consortia, however, have significant differences. The scope of the Global Partners Project prohibits an extensive discussion, so for brevity and consistency, only the Faculty Seminars, one part of each International Learning Center (designed to develop programs or develop interest in three different regions in which colleges in all three consortia wanted to explore), will be discussed.

The Faculty Seminars extend the familiar model of the faculty workshop. In the past, ACM had received a Ford Development Grant that allowed for extensive ongoing faculty workshops, so an administrative precedent existed. In the Global Partners Project, ACM has central responsibility for the Russia and Central Europe center, building on existing student academic programs located in Krasnodar, Russia, and Olomouc, Czech Republic.

During the spring and summer of 2001, an ACM faculty member conducted a seminar in East-Central Europe with ACM, ACS, and GLCA faculty members. Their specialties included literature, history, foreign languages, political science, environment studies, and education. The seminar focused specifically on Central European issues, and each faculty member developed an individual project. This model allowed faculty to create networks with consortia faculty as well as with faculty members and speakers in Central Europe.

The structure of the seminar enabled the group members to become acquainted with one another prior to their two and a half weeks in the Czech Republic. Before departure, the group met for a day to discuss the issues covered in their reading list. An e-mail list facilitated introductions and communication about shared interests. During the on-site workshop spent primarily in Olomouc, with a four-day excursion to Poland, the group members attended lectures, toured significant sites, and worked on individual projects.

This model of faculty collaboration is neither new nor innovative, but as a triconsortial activity, it has advantages for the participants. Unlike a seminar activity with participants from one campus, these faculty members were able to experiment with their ideas and interests free from the scrutiny and possibly judgment of their campus colleagues. Unlike a regional or national disciplinary conference, the participants met faculty members from different fields. And because of the similarities among ACM, GLCA, and ACS colleges, these faculty members share many of the same institutional experiences, a background that helped shape the topics covered in the seminar.

This faculty collaboration activity was also useful in supporting other activities of the consortium. One of the GLCA participants returned to the Czech Republic within a month to direct the ACM-GLCA Central European Program and felt that she had received the necessary background to fulfill her responsibilities; another ACM participant will direct it the next year, and several others intend to apply to direct it. The faculty benefited from the program by receiving support for their individual projects. One GLCA faculty member is returning for her sabbatical to continue work on her project, and others have remarked that the experience helped them to develop their research interests.

As the facilitator and the participants noted, ACM played an important logistical role in facilitating the interinstitutional faculty collaboration. First, a task force established the framework of the seminar, set guidelines for the participants, and provided a working model for the program. In addition, an administrative fellow at ACM, specifically hired with grant money, helped with the conceptual issues of the Global Partners Project as a whole and the Faculty Seminar as one part. ACM could rely on its colleagues at Palacky University, well known to it through the established program in Olomouc, who set up the lectures and worked to help the participants contact people in their specialties. Because this seminar was conducted at a program site, the consortium learned about the many resources available there; in addition, because of the contacts that the faculty made at the site, ACM has reconceptualized its relationship with the people at Palacky University, specifically considering new methods of faculty and student exchange.

Information Literacy Grant

In the fall of 2000, ACM received grant funding that explicitly supports activities across its member institutions to develop information literacy in several specific disciplines over a four-year period. The grant funds discipline-specific workshops that bring together faculty from the colleges of the consortium to work on projects to be incorporated in upper-level classrooms. The grant also funds meetings of ACM librarians and instructional technologists to create networks for sharing resources and aiding the faculty in their endeavors.

As the first grant activity, ACM sponsored a conference on information literacy at one of the consortial campuses. The sessions provided models for collaborative work in the area of information literacy as well as examples of particular projects. These collaborative projects were in general set on a single ACM campus. The challenge for the future grant activities is to establish interinstitutional relationships between faculty members, the librarians, and the instructional technologists.

As the first step after the conference, the ACM staff solicited suggestions for the workshops. In addition to being more time-consuming and drawn out than planned, the information-gathering process required some fine-tuning of the proposed grant activities. Initially, the ACM staff believed that the deans would be the primary source of information about the disciplines. They were a helpful beginning, but outreach needed to be extended. The process began by contacting the instructional technologists and librarians, who work directly with faculty members, and asked them to describe the information literacy work that they have done with different disciplines. The consortium then called the recommended faculty members and discussed possible projects with them.

The multifaceted process of gathering information led to modifications in the proposed grant activities. Many of the deans highlighted several of the restrictions—faculty responsibilities, differing institutional resources, and financial limitations—that complicate creating and maintaining faculty networks across the ACM institutions. The instructional technologists and librarians confirmed a growing suspicion that no discipline was appropriate for all the ACM campuses. The faculty highlighted the complexity and diversity of disciplines, a situation created by individual specialties, teaching responsibilities, department requirements, and institutional capacity. For example, some faculty members in psychology were primarily interested in developing the use of data sets in the classroom, while others were far more focused on library resources and bibliographic instruction.

In response to many of these comments, the ACM staff worked as a group to refine methods of presenting the collaborative activities. First, ACM sought, and found, a definition of information literacy that would fit, or at least not offend, all those involved in the grant. Also, in considering the issues of faculty time, the consortium discussed less ambitious projects and worked with faculty members to help them consider smaller projects that might begin as part of the grant activity and then be continued in some other form on their campuses. Responding to the financial concerns, ACM is still considering the possibility of using the funds to sponsor a smaller number of workshops. And instead of thinking broadly in disciplinary terms, it is now focusing on subgroups, such as American literature specialists rather than people in English departments. Methodological workshops may be another option—for example, the use of geographic information systems in the social sciences.

After six months of these discussions, economics was approved by the deans as one of the disciplinary workshops. A faculty member at one of the ACM colleges presented a proposal, and he will receive a stipend for organizing the workshops and coordinating the faculty and staff participation in the project. The ACM staff is helping him locate interested people in economics departments at the consortium colleges. He is also consulting with the instructional technologist and the reference librarian in the social sciences at his college to identify resources available for the use of the economists in developing their project.

The ACM Information Literacy project is in its early stages, but even in this exploratory period, the consortial office found organizing this interinstitutional faculty collaboration challenging. Because the grant did not specify any disciplines, ACM had the responsibility of assessing faculty development needs. This assessment required it to extend its traditional lines of communication. Also, as an issue coming up in the future, this workshop structure varies ACM's traditional model because the participants are not limited to one meeting; rather, the chosen faculty members will meet at least twice over two years. The workshops will result in a specific project, assignment, or outcome that can be shared with all the faculty and staff at ACM colleges, so the consortium, in conjunction with staff on the campuses, will be helping the participants locate the appropriate resources. The facilitators of the workshops will be both participants and coordinators of the long-distance activity that will occur during the meetings of the workshop. The consortium will need to help the workshop leader create an environment that sustains distance group work. With all of these factors to consider, the consortium staff will need to be flexible and adaptable in considering the needs of the specific groups.

Academic Collaboration Grant

In the fall of 2000, ACM received funds for faculty and curricular development through interinstitutional faculty collaboration. The projected outcome involves enhancing the liberal arts curriculum in traditional disciplines, an interdisciplinary area, or a specific methodology. Initially, the collaborative model included identifying specific leaders from the different campuses who would work with other committed faculty members.

Like the Information Literacy grant, this structure was reconfigured during the course of the conversation among the ACM deans. The deans proposed a wealth of ideas, such as theorizing computer science as a liberal art, providing aid for grant writing to faculty members in the sciences, creating models for interdisciplinary teaching, and discussing Midwest studies. After brainstorming different ideas, the deans shelved the debate so that they could return to their campuses and solicit suggestions from faculty members. They wanted tangible outcomes; they thought that the faculty members needed to place their energies in a project that would yield concrete results.

After a summer of informal discussions among the deans and faculty members at the ACM colleges, the deans proposed that the funds be used to support a three-year exploration of first-year programs. As many of the deans noted, concentrating on these programs would pull together faculty, librarians, student affairs staff, students, career development staff, instructional technologists, and administrators. The deans have several specific goals for this project, including sharing best practices, considering future directions, designing useful assessment models, and examining the sophomore year experience. A large conference, with a number of broad themes, will be held in the spring of 2003, and a series of smaller workshops and clustered activities will grow out of that conference.

This project, currently in planning stages, promises to carry both benefits and challenges. It allows for the individual campuses to introduce their own experiences to the rest of the institutions and to share experiences in order to address the students' academic, social, and personal progress. With the proposed structure of a big conference followed by a series of smaller gatherings, the Academic Collaboration grant builds on a familiar model; however, the time frame of the grant shifts the equation. Like so many other consortia, ACM generally works on finite projects rather than multiyear, multifaceted projects. With this initiative, ACM will be relying on the colleges to guide the consortium in sustaining the energy and enthusiasm of all the participants.

Consortial Issues in Fostering Faculty Collaboration

While each project contains its own specific virtues and challenges, some larger questions remain: What is involved in a consortium sponsoring interinstitutional faculty collaboration? How do the consortial colleges benefit? How does the consortium benefit from facilitating these types of initiatives?

The number of additional projects, in conjunction with the regular duties of the consortial staff, creates a strain for the consortial office. For the Global Partners Project, ACM hired an administrative fellow for two years. The person in that position worked solely on Global Partners matters. With the addition of the two other grants, the consortium hired another program officer for a longer duration. Duties and responsibilities were shifted in the consortial office so that the program officer had a range of responsibilities and was integrated within the consortial office. All change has its consequences, and ACM has had to be flexible and adaptable in working with each other as well as with the people at the ACM colleges.

Because these initiatives include external funding agents and, in the instance of the Global Partners Project, two other consortia, ACM has had to reconfigure internal lines of communication and consultation, an adaptation that has caused some tension between the consortial office and the deans. All the topics and projects originated on the consortial campuses, but as they moved into conference rooms with different participants, details were added and modified. Some of the changes took place in a time frame that did not allow for a great deal of consultation.

The deans were also concerned that the addition of so many faculty development projects shifted ACM's focus from administering student programs to facilitating faculty development and collaboration. Although they approved of the projects, the deans wanted to consider ACM's changing role. In the fall of 2001, ACM deans and presidents met for a retreat in which they discussed the benefits of participating in ACM initiatives and conceptualized some plans for the future. In many ways, this retreat alleviated some of the tension because ACM administrators were able to conceptualize their participation in these projects and set guidelines for the future.

Neither the deans nor the presidents questioned the value of ACM in fostering interinstitutional faculty collaboration. The colleges benefit by learning more about the resources available at the different colleges. That knowledge could potentially facilitate a greater sharing of resources, and it allows for an analysis of institutional capacity and culture. All of the ACM colleges retain their institutional autonomy and have distinct cultures. The faculty members, working in interinstitutional groups, are able to articulate and describe the specific culture of their campus, and that self-analysis becomes an important part of the project. The collaboration also provides faculty with a larger community, and the faculty members are able to envision larger projects with the support of a group, bringing those projects back to individual campuses.

ACM also profits from sponsoring interinstitutional faculty collaboration projects. The consortial staff are always responsible for educating people at the colleges about ACM's mission and activities. With these three projects, ACM has been able to contact and educate a significant number of people who had not previously participated in any ACM activities. With that education, the faculty members are more willing to explore other consortial activities. In addition, the consortium has learned more about events and activities, pedagogies, and practices that are occurring on the campuses. In creating these networks among faculty members across the ACM colleges, the consortium staff is also included in the network, and that inclusion will undoubtedly benefit future projects.

SARAH R. MARINO is program officer of the Associated Colleges of the Midwest in Chicago.

8

Library consortia are in a state of transformation as technology enables the development of virtual libraries while expanding opportunities for sharing printed works.

Academic Library Consortia in Transition

Ralph Alberico

Every academic library is part of an alliance that includes researchers, publishers, librarians, faculty, students, and funding agencies. Consortia, which involve groups of libraries cooperating for mutual benefit, are a natural outgrowth of a spirit of sharing that lies at the foundation of all libraries. Technology and economics are driving consortial activity in a new direction. An emerging mass audience has come to rely on library consortia as a reliable, trusted source of quality information. On many campuses, public and private, a consortium is the main source of digital collections offered by the library.

Consortia are assuming significant responsibility for managing electronic collections on behalf of states and nations. This chapter looks at examples drawn from the Virtual Library of Virginia (VIVA), a statewide consortium serving thirty-nine public institutions of higher education on fifty-two campuses and thirty-two private, nonprofit colleges and universities. VIVA serves a population of over 300,000 full-time-equivalent (FTE) students enrolled in academic programs, from certificate to postdoctoral. Consortia like VIVA are part of a larger set of library alliances, which represent many organizing principles and overlap and interact with one another as they coalesce toward a common point of view and delivery of services with regard to digital information streams.

Consortial Roles and Functions

Beyond the borrowing agreements made possible by shared on-line catalogues, consortia offer on-line collections that are equally and instantaneously available. Virtual library consortia focus on acquiring digital

New Directions for Higher Education, no. 120, Winter 2002 © Wiley Periodicals, Inc.

information. That focus includes providing on-line access and authenticating students and faculty. More recently, as the corpus of on-line information offered by consortia has grown, now including millions of journal articles available from some consortia, concerns about enabling resource discovery and promoting information literacy have come to the forefront.

Consortia provide large populations with access to digital information contained in massive, fluid collections. *Fluid* is the operative word. The scale of communities served by consortia and the scope of collections offered have implications for the marketplace and the polity. Consortia have become engaged, to a greater extent than in the past, in developing standards, policies, and business practices that underpin the foundation of academic libraries. Within higher education at the international level, library consortia have become players in a high-stakes game with profound programmatic and financial implications for most campuses.

Evolution of Library Consortia

The earliest academic library cooperatives were based on geographical proximity or shared mission. Projects supporting joint acquisitions, shared cataloguing, and reciprocal borrowing date back to the late nineteenth century (Weber, 1976). The first major growth wave of academic library consortia occurred in the 1960s, fueled by automation of cataloguing (Kopp, 1998). Library consortia were among the first institutions to take advantage of networked computing.

A new kind of digital library consortium arose in the 1990s (Allen and Hirshon, 1998). Rapid consolidation in the publishing industry and price escalation for research journals put libraries in the position of spending more and getting less. Statistics compiled by a group of more than 120 of the largest research libraries in North America show that overall expenditures on journal subscriptions increased by 192 percent between 1986 and 2000, while the consumer price index increased by only 57 percent. During the same period, the average cost for a journal subscription went up by 226 percent, while the number of titles purchased decreased by 7 percent (Kyrillidou and Young, 2001). A research library can easily spend millions of dollars on subscriptions, and the cost for a college library can run into hundreds of thousands of dollars annually. Yet it has been difficult to determine which items students and faculty actually use. The economics are untenable.

As the economic situation worsened, the Internet became the publishing medium for many forms of scholarly communication. Consortia, which aggregate on-line licenses for members, became an influential factor in the information marketplace. Potter (1997) analyzes VIVA and four other statewide academic library consortia and chronicles cooperative activities that would not be possible without the Internet.

VIVA was established in 1994 in response to a joint technology-based, cost-saving proposal from the academic library directors in Virginia and the higher education coordinating body, the State Council for Higher Education in Virginia. The history of VIVA reflects the evolution and development of similar consortia and is documented by Hurt (1994) and Perry (1995).

Benefits of Sharing

Consortia replace and complement functions once performed exclusively by individual libraries. Sharing of digital information is one characteristic of the new breed of consortium. Use of technology to enhance sharing of individual collections, for example, through electronic document delivery and on-line catalogues, is another. At the most fundamental level, VIVA is about two things: developing shared electronic collections and sharing the tangible items held by academic libraries in Virginia. Neither form of cooperation by itself is adequate to serve the needs of students and faculty. Thus, the mantra within VIVA and similar consortia is "more than a buying club."

There is no doubt that the unit cost of electronic information can be reduced significantly through consortial licenses. Within VIVA, financial benefits of consortial purchasing are at a five-to-one ratio, resulting in a cumulative cost avoidance of over $75 million since VIVA was established. Statewide licensing offers volume discounts. The economic benefit of VIVA is exemplified by the American Chemical Society journals. The 2001 subscription for this product cost VIVA $270,000 for public institutions in Virginia. If each public institution were to license the ACS journals independently, the cost would have been $1,477,000. Academic program planning at all public institutions can now take account of the fact that all the American Chemical Society journals are available on each campus at a reasonable cost. A community college student has the same opportunity for discovery as a student at a research university. Advantages of consortial membership go beyond pure economics.

Consortia reduce duplication of effort by negotiating standard license agreements to benefit members, reducing the need for each institution to manage complex contracts with multiple vendors. Consortia can coordinate technology investments and promote standards that facilitate sharing. They maximize use of existing library assets by promoting efficient sharing of items held by member libraries. Consortia have given academic libraries and their constituent institutions a greater voice in the market and political process. Finally, and perhaps most important, consortia can provide a baseline resource for everyone at each member institution.

From Infrastructure to Digital Collections

The bulk of VIVA's first appropriation, $5.2 million for the 1994–1996 biennium, was spent on infrastructure to provide members with basic capabilities required for virtual library initiatives. A whopping 56 percent of the initial budget was spent on hardware, with 38 percent allocated for collections. The long-range vision was of a digital library; hardware to support access in each member library was a necessary prerequisite.

Within a short time, emphasis and funding shifted. What began, before VIVA was founded, as a pilot resource-sharing project with the goal of a forty-eight-hour turnaround time on sending copies of journal articles became a large-scale licensing enterprise. Expenditures moved from infrastructure to electronic content. Content investments moved from secondary information such as indexing and abstracting services to electronic journals. By the 2000–2002 biennium, the VIVA budget had increased to $10.7 million, with 88 percent spent on electronic collections and zero on hardware.

Governance, Administration, and Funding

New library consortia defy easy categorization. There is wide variation in funding, governance, and operations. Perhaps the most critical factor is the level of centralization. Some consortia receive most of their funding from a central agency; others are funded primarily by contributions from members. Some assume central responsibility for managing information services; others contract that responsibility out to information service providers. Consortia also vary in terms of the types of institutions represented in their membership and the extent to which operations are centralized or distributed. In most cases, consortia deal with representatives of member institutions rather than directly with students and faculty. As they operate at higher levels, a common strategy for addressing scaling issues is a consortium of consortia, in which the higher-level organization deals only with other consortia. For example, Groen (2000) describes the Canadian National Site Licensing Project, which is spending $50 million over a three-year period on behalf of Consortia Canada, a consortium of fourteen academic library consortia.

VIVA is an example of a centrally funded organization in which most of the on-line collections and much of the work is distributed. VIVA members include nonprofit higher education institutions in Virginia, with benefits accruing equally to each public institution: twenty-four community colleges, nine comprehensive colleges and universities, and six doctoral institutions.

Independent (private) schools in Virginia, which also participate in VIVA, may elect to take advantage of discounted licenses individually or by pooling their own funds. As VIVA matured, the state began providing collection funding for private institutions on a matching basis. Funding provided by private schools is supplemented on a two-to-one ratio by state funds. In the 2000–2002 biennium, the pool consisted of $375,000: $250,000 from the state and $125,000 supplied by thirty of thirty-two private schools that chose to contribute. The Virginia Independent College and

University Library Association, which functions in some respects as a consortium within the larger consortium, makes decisions on use of pooled funds. The independent institutions are full partners in VIVA interlibrary loan agreements. VIVA provides software and technical support to public and private schools alike for electronic delivery of journal articles.

Private institutions add to collective purchasing power, share items from their collections, reduce pressure on public institutions in the state, and play an important role in garnering political support. Their participation has been critical to the success of VIVA. All institutions—public, private, community college, and research university—play a role in governance of the consortium and in contributing to its work.

A Complex Organizational Matrix

Personnel funded by VIVA include two full-time positions: a project director with an administrative assistant who are located at George Mason University and 6.5 FTE support personnel at other institutions. Personnel support for procurement services resides at James Madison University, and fewer than one FTE classified staff at each of the six largest libraries help to support document delivery among members. The role of the project director has been critical to VIVA's success; the job requires negotiating skills, financial savvy, a political sense, and the ability to handle the myriad tasks associated with management of the enterprise.

Additional personnel support comes from four committees and volunteers whose labor is contributed by their home institutions. This ensures that the consortium serves the interests of its members. VIVA is staffed by a cadre of librarians representative of the full spectrum of institutional types in the consortium. Those people, each employed by a different institution, act as agents of the consortium. The project director coordinates the effort.

VIVA is decentralized technologically as well as administratively. Databases are generally not maintained on servers managed by the consortium. Instead, VIVA provides its members with access to collections maintained on vendor Web sites. This gets VIVA out of the business of managing centralized database production servers, significantly reducing administrative overhead. This is offset to a certain extent by platform fees charged by vendors for hosting information content purchased by the consortium.

The combination of central funding and distributed responsibility reflects an organizational model based on interinstitutional teams. Working relationships stress collaboration across institutions. The result is an organizational matrix in which contact with colleagues in other institutions can be as frequent and meaningful as interactions with colleagues at home. Work done on behalf of the consortium is recognized and rewarded on member campuses.

Distributed Labor

A consistent goal of VIVA has been to keep administrative overhead low. VIVA exemplifies a lean committee structure, reflecting an agreement among member libraries to share the work. Governance is vested in a steering committee with representatives of each type of institution. Primary tasks are carried out by a small central administration and three standing committees: the Resource Sharing Committee, the Resources for Users Committee, and the Outreach Committee, each with fewer than a dozen members who are also representatives of member institutions. The Steering Committee must approve financial commitments and matters of policy.

The Resources for Users Committee is charged with identifying, evaluating, recommending, and supporting digital collections, including approximately two hundred databases and over ten thousand full-text journals and newspapers. This committee oversees transactions that approached $9 million in the 2000–2002 biennium. The Resource Sharing Committee is charged with addressing issues related to borrowing and lending among member libraries. The Outreach Committee publicizes VIVA resources to the academic community and promotes integration of digital collections with curricula on each campus. Other committees are convened on a periodic basis, for example, to address technical and training issues that do not require ongoing attention from a standing committee.

Approximately 1 percent of the budget is spent on travel and training. This supplements the labor contribution from each school and enables work to be coordinated. For example, the Resources for Users Committee sponsors training on a regular basis to familiarize members with new on-line services. Attendees, who receive modest travel support, apply the training to supporting students and faculty on their own campuses. For a consortium that relies on donated labor from member institutions, this support is critical.

A Constellation of Trust Relationships

The entire community is polled electronically on a periodic basis for evaluative input on potential purchases. Data on resource use are available in a secure location to all consortium members. Indexes, journals, and reference works licensed by the consortium are reviewed on a periodic basis. Database directories, library directories, links to each library's on-line catalogue, contact lists for key people in each library, special interest listservs, vendor contacts, and technical support material are maintained by the consortium. A common pool of information managed by consortium members drives decisions. Volunteers handle preliminary license negotiations; broad input and data are gathered to support each decision and disseminated through channels maintained by the consortium. Central staff handles final negotiations, and recommendations are approved by the steering committee.

An effective consortium becomes the center of a constellation of trust relationships. Members trust the consortium to provide resources and services for academic programs on their campuses. Students and faculty trust the quality of the digital information available from their libraries. The consortium trusts its members to contribute to the cooperative effort. Vendors trust the consortium to enforce restrictions on access, and the consortium trusts vendors to deliver information content and services as promised. Many of these trust relationships are embodied in contracts and technical authentication systems. Others are reflected in formal and informal agreements among members. A memorandum of understanding specifies obligations and responsibilities of members. Other agreements, such as an interlibrary loan protocol in which members agree to expedite turnaround time on requests, provide guidelines on interaction within the consortium.

Funding Incentives

Members of a library consortium operate in enlightened self-interest. The funding agency provides incentives for cooperation; the governing structure in turn provides further incentives. One significant aspect of VIVA is that the consortium is funded by the state legislature; its budget shows up as a line item in legislative appropriations. The bulk of funding is provided by the state rather than by members.

Use of institutional pooled funds, which VIVA has tried for some collection projects, does not yield the same results as use of centrally allocated funds. For projects in which members are asked to contribute local funds, there is much greater emphasis on support for local needs. Decisions on use of central funds tend to emphasize resources that serve the largest number of students and faculty across institutions. Many consortia have been in a growth mode since the 1990s. Yet even during periods of growth, it has been rare for public institutions to see state funds flowing toward consortia and individual libraries at the same time. In Virginia, VIVA funding has increased as materials budgets in the majority of individual member libraries have remained flat. OhioLINK, by many measures the most ambitious of the new generation of academic library consortia, was founded on the premise that on-line services provided by the consortium would obviate the need for capital investments in library buildings (Potter, 1997)

Collection Sharing

Resource sharing has been a major impetus for growth of consortia and remains important even for consortia whose main work is developing digital collections. Within Virginia, there is a huge investment in library collections built up over more than three hundred years. Funds that VIVA provides to support resource-sharing activities ($700,000 or about 7 percent of the VIVA budget for the 2000–2002 biennium) are relatively small when compared to the investments made in acquiring digital collections. Library-sharing cooperatives rely on the fact that each library has unique items, which can be shared with others, and each scholar requires a unique set of resources. When it comes to sharing collections, a minimal investment on the part of the consortium yields a large return for students and faculty who have access to items from each member library.

Consortia and Electronic Publishing

A goal of early collection development agreements among libraries was to cover the territory by avoiding duplication. In a digital world, the goal is to democratize access. Publishers offer site licensing deals for their entire catalogues, and libraries band together to license digital collections. There is high overlap among electronic collections, which are more easily shared across institutions than print collections are. The packages in which information is delivered have changed, as have publishing entities and consumer entities. Consortia are purchasing entire electronic journal collections for hundreds of thousands of dollars at the same time they are contracting for blocks of individual searches at around sixty cents each.

Most electronic journal publishers are grounded in print publishing, and initial business models did not reflect the realities of an on-line marketplace. An economic goal for publishers is to protect the revenue streams generated by paper journal subscriptions while making investments needed to enter electronic markets. For consortia, the goal is to offer more information to more people for less money.

A consortium like VIVA manages contracts that include many permutations of cost factors, terms, and conditions. Factors such as FTE enrollment play a major role in most contracts. In addition to negotiating contracts whose terms are favorable to members, consortia often develop multiple costing models, which are used to determine the level of contribution that members are assessed for shared costs. Factors that influence pricing by vendors are also used on a case-by-case basis to determine members' shares of deals that involve local monies.

While financial advantage is a powerful motivator, expanding access to information is even more powerful. In the end, it is not economies of scale but expanded access that matters most—not the big deal, in other words, but the big audience that goes with it. On any campus, availability of information resources factors into academic program decision making and accreditation processes; absence of core titles can forestall new programs. On campuses where there is a large pool of shared digital resources, curriculum development can be more flexible.

In addition to adding flexibility to academic program development on local campuses, a consortium can provide a baseline knowledge resource in support of collaborative distance-learning programs. In Virginia, VIVA works closely with the Electronic Campus of Virginia, the statewide distance-learning group.

Near-universal on-line access leads to new patterns of use, and for the first time, use can be accurately measured. Campuses have become consumer oriented, network oriented, and self-service. Without accurate use statistics, it is impossible to understand the needs of students and faculty who use the on-line library more than they use the physical library. These data provide metrics for making decisions about digital collections and help each campus understand which sources are most important to its students and faculty. Standard ways of defining and measuring the use of electronic information are important to consortia. Publishers that fail to provide use statistics risk losing consortial business.

Resource Discovery

Each library in VIVA integrates electronic services from the consortium with its own Web site. Whether a specific on-line journal or reference source is provided locally or from the consortium is transparent to users. As digital collections grow, consortia are beginning to contend with resource discovery issues. There is a separate access path and user interface to the offerings of each vendor, and in a volatile market, the vendor for any given journal or reference service changes often. There is no single integrated collection; there are many collections, each with its own title list and idiosyncrasies. Natural relationships between and among items in separate collections are difficult to discover. Consortia are just beginning to develop resource discovery tools and access strategies that promote exploration and allow scholars to establish connections across collections.

There is a long way to go before digital collections become digital libraries. One challenge is building sustainable digital archives in which important scholarly information is preserved for future researchers. Consortia are already working with publishers on overcoming legal and technical barriers to meet the challenge; long-term preservation of the digital record can come only from a truly monumental cooperative effort.

Libraries are working together in new and innovative ways, providing on-line services that support academic programs and making decisions that maximize access to the best digital information. Consortia are perfecting ongoing support for large communities. As the audience gets bigger and on-line collections grow, consortia will get even better at removing the barriers between electronic collections and seekers of knowledge.

References

Allen, B. M., and Hirshon, A. "Hanging Together to Avoid Hanging Separately: Opportunities for Academic Libraries and Consortia." *Information Technology and Libraries*, 1998, 17(1), 36–45.

Groen, F. "Funding Innovation in Canadian Research Libraries: A National Initiative to Advance Access to Electronic Journals and Information." In *Proceedings of the Eighth International Congress on Medical Librarianship.* London: International Congress on Medical Internship, 2000. [http://www.icml.org/monday/future/groen.htm].

Hurt, C. "Building the Foundations of Virginia's Virtual Library." *Virginia Librarian,* 1994, *40*(3), 12–15.

Kopp, J. J. "Library Consortia and Information Technology: The Past, the Present, the Promise." *Information Technology and Libraries,* 1998, *17*(1), 7–12.

Kyrillidou, M., and Young, M. (comps.). *ARL Statistics, 1999–2000.* Washington, D.C.: Association of Research Libraries, 2001. [http://www.arl.org/stats/arlstat/00pub/00arlstat.pdf].

Perry, K. "VIVA's First Year." *Virginia Librarian,* 1995, *41*(4), 14–16.

Potter, W. G. "Recent Trends in Statewide Academic Library Consortia." *Library Trends,* 1997, *45*(3), 416–435.

Weber, D. C. "A Century of Cooperative Programs Among Academic Libraries." *College and Research Libraries,* 1976, *37*(3), 205–221.

RALPH ALBERICO *is dean of libraries and educational technologies at James Madison University in Harrisonburg, Virginia, and chair of the Virtual Library of Virginia steering committee.*

9

Collaborative efforts among institutions serving the same clientele have become an economic necessity in educational programming; however, successful partnering requires careful planning.

SUNY Colleges in the North Country: A Successful Partnership with the Military

Joanne Y. Corsica, Donald R. Johnson, Wanda Rushing Lancaster

The SUNY Colleges in the North Country Consortium, established in 1985, is situated in a rural area of northern New York, hundreds of miles from New York City, more than seventy miles from the nearest four-year college campus, and geographically isolated several months of the year due to severe winter weather conditions. Imagine the impact on this bucolic region in 1985 when the U.S. Army announced that Jefferson County would become home to a new infantry division. Suddenly every facet of life was significantly affected, especially higher education. Prior to 1985, only two institutions had served the area: Jefferson Community College and a small unit of State University of New York (SUNY) Empire State College. After the activation of the new army division and a subsequent population growth of roughly thirty thousand people, the need for additional higher educational opportunities became a clear priority for the military and the surrounding community.

Realizing that construction of a new campus was not an economically viable option, regional institution presidents, leaders from the army's Fort Drum, and the SUNY provost formulated the idea of a collaborative initiative to address higher education needs. This initiative evolved into a new organization, the SUNY Colleges of the North County, to be collocated with the Army Education Center on the new Fort Drum military installation near Watertown.

The SUNY Colleges in the North Country comprises nine member institutions committed to working collaboratively: Jefferson Community

College, College of Technology at Canton, Empire State College (ESC), College of Environmental Science and Forestry, Institute of Technology-Utica/Rome, Oswego State College, Plattsburgh State College, Potsdam College, and Upstate Medical University. Governance is provided by a board of directors consisting of a representative appointed by each college president. The board sets policy and gives direction to the executive director, who is responsible for day-to-day organizational operations. A support staff handles the reception, registration, and office duties. Faculty advisers represent their individual campuses and provide advisement and instructional services to students.

Unlike most other military installations where there are several competing colleges, each with a separate representative, the consortium represents several cooperating colleges and uses its executive director as the primary liaison with the military.

The relationship between Fort Drum and the consortium is outlined in a memorandum of understanding signed by the Fort Drum garrison commander and the chair of the consortium board of directors. According to its terms, Army Education Services staff counsel and evaluate soldiers on educational and career goals, objectives, and programs. In addition, Fort Drum provides consortium members with office space, classrooms, and various laboratory facilities.

Consortium Cooperation: Best Practices

Consortium cooperation has ameliorated intercollege competition, minimized confusing intercollege paperwork requirements, and enhanced the educational opportunities and learning experiences for all students by sharing college resources. The close working relationships developed among the various faculties and staffs have helped each member institution's programs to grow in a way that would have been impossible had they operated as single entities. Furthermore, the cooperative working relationships that have developed among member schools and between consortium faculties and Fort Drum education services staff have enhanced the quality of work life for all involved. More important, these relationships have allowed all academic players to put the student in the center of the learning process.

Following are some of the best practices the consortium has developed to meet the educational needs of the collective study body:

• *Flexible and creative schedules.* Courses are formatted in a variety of time frames to align with military training schedules and deployments, thus maximizing opportunities for student participation.
• *Cooperative advisement.* The college advisers work in cooperative, facilitative ways to provide students with the most effective and expedient (in terms of meeting degree requirements) options to enroll in courses. Rather than acting in a competitive, enrollment-driven manner, the consortium

advisers often guide a student to enroll in a course with one of the other consortium institutions because that course is a better fit with the student's ultimate educational goals and time constraints.

• *Sharing of faculty resources.* In a region that is mostly rural, the availability of qualified instructors is limited. Direct communication among member institutions has facilitated the staffing of courses that might have been canceled or not even scheduled, thus expanding course opportunities for students.

• *Cross-enrollments.* The consortium institutions have worked together to make cross-registrations easier for students. After a cross-registration form is submitted to an institution, that school's bursar sends a bill back to the student's home institution for tuition payment.

• *Transfer of financial aid.* Formal cross-registration among institutions makes the process of applying financial aid to outside enrollments much easier. A student's financial aid award is posted to the tuition or fee bill at the home institution. Included in the total is the amount that the home college will send to the other institution to cover the cross-registration costs.

• *Creative course schedules.* The consortium institutions create course schedules designed to meet the needs of both the individual college's students and the students of the other member institutions, thus allowing a greater range of course selections than any single institution could offer.

The primary mission of the SUNY Colleges of the North Country is putting the student first and in the center of learning. When all of the member institutions are focused on this goal, then the unique, parochial differences of the institutions, which could become stumbling blocks, become instead salient, positive assets to the total educational opportunities for all students. Partnerships have always been effective in the delivery of education services; in a time of reduced resources and increased demands for services, fostering effective partnerships among institutions is not only wise but essential.

Each of the consortium members brings unique educational programs and services to students. For example, Jefferson Community College offers lower-division liberal arts, business, and criminal justice courses in three-week to eight-week intensive instructional blocks. These blocks are structured to be congruent with military training schedules and held in both the Army Education Center and unit classrooms around the installation. Similarly, the College of Technology at Canton offers abbreviated, intensive upper-division courses in criminal investigation. Canton has also conducted automotive mechanics courses in unit motor pools. ESC provides a nontraditional alternative to classroom-based instruction with its mentor-guided, independent study model. It offers opportunities for students to develop individualized liberal arts and business courses of study and degree programs outside traditional academic terms at the associate, baccalaureate, and graduate levels. Oswego State College offers classroom term-based upper-division and graduate-level liberal arts and business courses. Plattsburgh State College offers a bachelor of science in nursing through teleconferencing using distance-learning facilities at Jefferson Community College's main campus. Potsdam College is the primary provider of graduate-level education courses. Consortium institutions also offer a myriad of distance-learning courses and degrees by teleconferencing, paper-based courses, and the Internet to enhance student access to learning opportunities.

Case Studies

The case studies that follow reflect educational paths that students might take in using the unique features of the various consortium institutions (they do not represent actual students).

• Sergeant Jones is an infantryman who had no prior college experience when he was assigned to Fort Drum. His first exposure to college was through intensive unit courses conducted by Jefferson Community College in Jones's company and battalion classrooms. He also was able to complete several on-post evening courses. Once he applied for admission to Jefferson, the college evaluated his military training and experience for credit. After taking advantage of a Fort Drum reenlistment option to attend college full time for one semester, he earned his associate degree in individual studies. Jones then chose to continue his education with one of the consortium's four-year colleges to pursue a business degree. Due to a demanding work schedule and periodic deployments, ESC's nonclassroom-based instruction mode was the most practical choice for him. He could begin a semester when it was convenient for him and work with a mentor on-site or at a distance. At various times, Jones wanted, and was able, to enroll through cross-registration in classroom-based business courses with both Potsdam and Oswego State colleges. When he was deployed to Bosnia, he continued his ESC courses through distance learning. On his return to Fort Drum, he completed his remaining degree requirements and earned his bachelor of science degree in business.

• Staff Sergeant Brown is a military police officer who came to Fort Drum having completed some prior college course work in liberal arts and criminal justice areas; however, she lacked a degree. Brown decided to complete her associate degree in criminal justice with Jefferson Community College and her bachelor's degree with Oswego State. She did so understanding that she would be able to access Canton's unique criminal investigation courses and ESC's mentor-guided courses in criminology and sociology through the cross-registration process.

• Yolanda Gonzales, the wife of an army captain, recently arrived at Fort Drum. She holds a bachelor's degree in business and has decided to change career paths. She now wants to become a certified elementary school teacher. To do so in New York State, she must complete state-mandated courses and fulfill student teaching obligations. After consulting with the Potsdam College adviser at Fort Drum, Gonzales learned that a master's degree is required for permanent certification in New York. To qualify for Potsdam's master of science in teaching program, she would need to take additional undergraduate courses in liberal arts and foreign language. She has three children at home and is not able to attend campus-based courses at the Potsdam College main campus, seventy miles from Fort Drum. The Potsdam adviser referred her to Jefferson Community College and ESC for advisement regarding the completion of the needed undergraduate courses. These colleges offer alternative instructional delivery modes, such as shorter-term on-post courses and guided independent study options. Gonzales has been able to pursue her educational goals while still meeting her family responsibilities. Once she completes her undergraduate courses, she will be able to enroll in the master of science in teaching degree through Potsdam's Fort Drum area graduate courses.

Partnering with the Army

SUNY Colleges of the North Country Consortium consists of a multilayer of partnerships. The nine-member consortium is a partnership within SUNY and a partnership between SUNY and Fort Drum. As a function of the military partnership, all member colleges participate in the Servicemembers Opportunity Colleges Army Degree (SOCAD) program, itself a partnership of 140 two-year and four-year colleges offering degree programs on army installations around the world.

The SUNY consortium advisers and staff work closely with army education counselors in guiding students into appropriate degree programs. At the formation of the SUNY Consortium partnership with Fort Drum, the basic assumption underlying the initiative was that member institutions would get increased enrollments, generating higher levels of income, and the army would get better educational services. The reality of the partnership is that the increased enrollments are directly attributable to positive cooperation rather than parochial competition. The partnership with the army has facilitated and enhanced the positive cooperation between schools because army education counselors do not represent any one institution but are advocates for their soldier-students. This nesting of multilayered partnerships keeps the focus on the students' educational needs and objectives, placing them in the center of their learning.

What Works

In analyzing why the consortium has been so successful in its relationship with the military, it is important to understand the historical relationship between the military at Fort Drum and the three-county region in which it is based. Prior to the Department of the Army's decision to reactivate the

Tenth Mountain Division and locate it at Fort Drum, the North Country area as a whole was experiencing significant and substantial job loss and economic distress. Clearly understanding the positive economic impact that the Tenth Mountain Division could have on the area, public officials in the three-county area worked closely with the military leaders in building a wide range of partnerships. One of the first and most significant of these partnerships involved locating military housing units throughout the region. Not only did this encourage the military in establishing and building relationships with the communities, but it also engaged the communities in multiple layers of interaction and partnering with the military. The expansion brought jobs, services, and opportunities for growth to declining communities. A major focus of the services was an expansion of educational services and opportunities to school-aged children and varied college-level populations as well. Essentially, the consortium was able to establish its partnership with the military within the exiting relationships forged between the military and the community.

The effectiveness of this consortium is a function of strong administrative leadership at the top. Such leadership is needed to initiate partnering efforts in spite of the risks that interinstitutional cooperation might entail. An example is letting other institutions obtain enrollments; coming up against entrenched tenured faculty who oppose changes in delivery models such as structure of terms, off-campus course locations, and use of adjunct instructors; and adapting to the needs of adult students. Sustained commitment and vision on the part of all players (military leaders, college administrators, on-site institutional advisers and educators, and army education counselors) is necessary to build campus support with college academic departments, registrars, bursars, admissions, and financial aid offices. Such commitment is also necessary to build support with the multiple layers of military leadership, for example, a soldier's chain of command. On-site college staff need to be student focused, nonparochial, and noncompetitive in serving their individual students and in representing their respective institutions. The staff who are the senior in experience are more effective in facilitating campuswide support for the consortium's collaborative design and mission.

The SUNY consortium's college staff are an integral part of various North Country communities and have many developed long-term service relationships within those communities. For example, consortium personnel have held local political offices, served on community services boards, conducted training with local law enforcement agencies, taught in local public school systems, and owned local businesses. This integration allows them to enhance the learning experiences of military students by linking them directly to appropriate community resources; a majority of the consortium staff are graduates of the Chamber of Commerce's Leadership Institute. In addition, the consortium staff and affiliated college leaders are actively involved with local military-community groups such as the

Association of the United States Army and the Fort Drum Regional Liaison Organization.

The consortium provides noncompetitive course and degree offerings that complement and supplement each other's programs. For example, Jefferson Community College added the Elementary Spanish 1 and 2 courses to its Fort Drum schedule to assist Potsdam students in meeting foreign language requirements for teacher certification. ESC offers upper-division sociology courses for Canton College of Technology's criminal investigation bachelor's degree program and for Oswego College's bachelor's degree in public justice. ESC students can cross-register with Jefferson for laboratory science requirements. Jefferson Community College has partnered with the consortium's institutions offering baccalaureate degrees in creating jointly matriculated degree programs allowing a student to be accepted at two institutions and two degree levels at the same time. Member schools are jointly marketed and share office equipment, support staff, and faculty resources. Often faculty advisers consult with each other concerning the best institutional and degree program for a particular student and then guide that student to another college's office. Given the complementary nature of the programs, the consortium is able to offer every learning modality to students: classroom based, distance learning, and guided independent study.

The SUNY consortium's relationship with Fort Drum is an excellent example of the reciprocal relationships necessary for an effective and successful partnership. Give-and-take economics are a major part of this reciprocity. For instance, Fort Drum provides the consortium office space, classrooms, furniture, computer labs, instructional technology, Internet linkage, utilities, and library services without cost to member institutions. In turn, the consortium provides immediate, face-to-face student problem resolution, on-site advising and information, quality educational services and programming, and special request courses. In addition, the consortium partially funds library staff positions at both the Fort Drum Library and Jefferson Community College's main campus library.

The result of this successful partnership is clearly reflected in the enrollment growth of member institutions. In 1985, the consortium's first year of operation, unduplicated enrollments totaled 587. Enrollment numbers have been steadily increasing and in fiscal year 2000–1 exceeded five thousand. Course offerings have grown from an initial offering of 55 in 1985 to a high of 236. Consortium office staff have grown from two full-time staff housed in a one-room office to a staff of twelve housed in a multioffice complex.

Conclusion

Collaborative efforts have become an economic necessity in educational programming; however, successful partnering does not just happen. There are several critical factors involved in the creation and ongoing maintenance of such relationships:

- Partnerships must be practical. Because of unique geographical, climatic, and economic factors, partnerships can often deliver a service that may not be otherwise available due to distance, bad weather, and work schedules.
- Partnerships must be cost-effective. They can deliver services that otherwise might not be economically feasible for a single entity in a sparsely populated rural area.
- Partnerships must be a model for good public relations. A well-planned partnership demonstrates to the public that their educational needs are being met in a responsible, cost-effective manner.
- Innovative collaborations must be based on clearly identified needs and reasonable opportunities.
- Whole-campus commitment to interschool cooperation is critical. No single department or institution can or should attempt to provide agreed-on services and support.
- Consortium partners must embrace institutional flexibility in spite of ingrained institutional traditions.
- A solid funding base is indispensable. In order to provide effective and strategically planned programs as well as an extended commitment to a body of students, organizational stability must be provided through adequate and consistent funding.
- A dynamic philosophy that includes vision and creativity in strategic planning should be a vital and ongoing part of the partnership.
- Successful partnerships require an excellent educational product. Academic reputation through word of mouth has been the consortium's most effective marketing tool.

The SUNY Colleges in the North Country has had a solid fifteen-year history of success in its relationship with the military at Fort Drum, as demonstrated by its exponential program and enrollment growth. Such student-centered partnerships between the military and institutions of higher learning can make a positive difference in the lives of students and the communities in which they live.

JOANNE Y. CORSICA is program coordinator for the Fort Drum Unit of SUNY Empire State College, Saratoga Springs, New York.

DONALD R. JOHNSON is extension site coordinator at Fort Drum for Jefferson Community College, Watertown, New York.

WANDA RUSHING LANCASTER is executive director for the SUNY Colleges in the North Country, Fort Drum, New York.

10

Purchasing as a profession has changed from buying things to managing processes, and the change has enhanced the use of consortium or group purchasing as a cost-effective tool.

Consortium Purchasing

Jake E. Bishop

During the past few years, purchasing as a profession has evolved from one of buying things to managing processes. With cuts in higher education and administrative redesign prevalent, educational purchasing agents find themselves managing processes and major contracts, while end users are empowered to do more of the day-to-day buying themselves.

Purchasing departments in higher education now have responsibility for on-line ordering systems, procurement cards, contract creation and management, asset management, accounts payable, policy and procedures, training, leasing, contracts for services, construction, maintenance repair, and major bids. At some institutions, purchasing responsibility may extend to central receiving, stores, mail, copy centers, vending, outsourcing project management, and surplus property and property rentals. Doing more with less is the order of the day. Consequently, purchasing departments have had to develop new and better methods while efficiently supporting the institution's mission. One important way of doing this is participation in group or consortium purchasing.

This is not a new idea. Hospital purchasing groups and the Educational and Institutional Cooperative Service date back over sixty-five years. The depression and World War II were major stimuli for the cooperative movement. The history of the United States in fact points to the consortium tradition. The pilgrims who arrived on the *Mayflower* were a consortium of sorts. A consortium is effective when the people who join together accomplish what none of them could do individually. Wagon trains, barn raisings, husking and quilting bees, farm co-ops, credit unions, cooperative banks, and insurance companies were all logical next steps. This has led to contemporary examples: condominiums, timeshares, food co-ops, health maintenance organizations, academic consortia, and purchasing consortia. This is not limited to higher education. Consider drugstore, hardware, discount, and grocery store chains where the store is independent but the group joins together to buy in bulk.

There is great diversity in size among colleges and universities. A small, religious school or a community college that does not house and feed students does not have the budget or buying power of a large research university. The synergism of working together suggests that the whole can accomplish more than any of the parts.

Why Purchasing Consortia Form

Institutions in close proximity have long histories of shared courses and professors, shared libraries, feeding operations, bus services, computer networks, cooperation in admissions, identification cards, and joint academic programs. This naturally led to other departments working together: the bursars, human resources, physical plants, public safety, insurance, and procurement. In smaller institutions, there may be a business manager with a number of responsibilities, with purchasing being only one of them. Contrast this with larger institutions that have separate purchasing departments with a staff of purchasing professionals, and the variations in availability of time, expertise, and experience become clear.

The sharing of responsibility can lead to a streamlining of the buying process, greater continuity and consistency, and economies of scale. When purchasing people meet, they can share experience and expertise, reduce paperwork, provide faster response time to end users, and save real dollars by combining their buying power and creating broad-based, longer-term contracts. This working together will also free people up to handle larger projects where they can add more value than they do processing small orders. Small orders are most common in higher education. Unlike an assembly line that is turning out the same product over and over again, higher education is involved in teaching, experimentation, and pure research. Where the industrial purchasing agent will buy ten thousand of one item, the purchasing agent in higher education buys one of a thousand different items. People doing research may try hundreds of things before they find the one that works.

A few years ago, the University of Massachusetts did a study of what it costs to process small orders. Purchase orders and requisitions were followed from the inception of an idea, through preparation, mail, processing, delivery, invoicing, and payment. Average clerical, administrative, and faculty salaries were used to determine hourly rates. Each step in the process was tracked, and time and cost were assigned to handling each step. The outcome determined that every order followed sixty-eight distinct hands-on steps and that it cost $113 to process each order regardless of size. Amazingly, higher education often spends more on administrative process than it does on the goods.

This finding was so alarming that other institutions, agencies, and businesses were surveyed to see if the cost per order could possibly be correct. From a low of $75 per order, costs to process ranged up to $600, with the average at $100 to $150. Knowing the data were correct, the University of Massachusetts moved aggressively to the use of procurement credit cards. Most schools have done the same, for administrators and purchasing agents add no value to the handling of small transactions.

This is not a small problem. At the time, the University of Massachusetts was processing seventy-seven thousand purchase orders per year to buy $136 million in goods and services. Even more revealing, only eighteen thousand of those orders accounted for $126 million of the total spent; the other fifty-nine thousand purchase orders totaled only $10 million. Small orders averaged only $168 while costing $113 to handle. Use of the procurement card reduced the processing steps to twelve and the cost to process to a few dollars. It is no wonder that institutions now commonly have hundreds of these cards in use on campus. An obvious secondary benefit is quicker response time to end user needs and faster payment for vendors.

Most purchasing consortia create contracts that require vendors to accept credit cards for ordering and payment. Consequently, purchasing contracts not only help reduce the price for quality products, they streamline the process and help with the handling of small transactions. Group purchasing is often looked on very favorably by auditors and accreditation teams because it demonstrates good business practices and creates a more auditable paper trail.

Regional Consortia Versus National Consortia

Colleges and universities may feel more comfortable with regional consortia than they do with nationwide consortia. Proximity makes it easier for partners to get together on a regular basis. Regular member meetings are very important because they provide a forum for conducting business, taking votes, sharing information, and discussing new contracts. Those who live in a region speak the same language (some even have the same accent), share a culture and philosophy that is more common, and share experience with local and regional vendors. A network extends beyond meetings to the sharing of information, specifications, and answers on an ongoing basis.

Regular consortium meetings can provide an opportunity for professional development as well. This may consist of a lecture, demonstration, or seminar, or it may involve a factory tour, showroom tour, or even the tour of a new building constructed by a member. Seeing how others have used technology or space may save an institution from making the same mistake or help in finding a solution.

Many groups hold product shows that bring the contract vendors together for an exhibit. The opportunity for people from all segments of member campuses to visit one place for a few hours to see a large number of vendors and their products could not be replicated with many trips on many days.

Open information exchanges can become real brainstorming, problem-solving forums. Sometimes we forget that avoidance of repeating an error is as much an institutional cost avoidance as the saving of dollars through discounts. Managing a localized regional consortium will have lower overhead than trying to manage a group that is nationwide.

What a Consortium Does

A common misconception is that purchasing consortia buy things. That is usually not the case. The member schools and end users do the buying direct from vendors, maintaining the customer-vendor relationship. The consortium will intercede only if there is a problem: someone does not deliver, or someone fails to pay a bill. What a consortium does do is streamline the process, saving ten, twenty, or fifty schools from replicating the contract work over and over again. The reduction of the administrative burden will no doubt equal the bottom-line dollars saved through better discounts and pricing. Creation and management of shared contracts and their distribution, on-line or on paper, account for 75 percent of a consortium's time. Collecting data, running meetings, and reporting account for the other 25 percent.

Consortia bring joint buying power to bear on the marketplace. They act as agent for the members and create an auditable paper trail. They also prequalify vendors to be bidders, mediate and resolve problems, and help members avoid errors and the replication of work. This frees people to work on projects where their time and talent can have more impact.

Through ease of record keeping and staff, a purchasing consortium can promote environmentally conscious procurement and recycling and promote the use of minority, woman-owned, small, disadvantaged businesses and correctional industries. For public institutions, it can be the vehicle that conducts public sealed bids on which national consortia, with negotiated contracts, can bid.

Today in purchasing, total cost of acquisition is the focus. From inception of an idea for a need to acquisition, lifetime use and operation, and disposal, we need to focus more on total cost over time, life cycle value, and the freeing up of staff to work on bigger tasks where they can add real value. Moreover, requiring a professor, researcher, or high-level administrator to find and purchase an item is not necessarily a good use of their time or what they were hired to do. To spend $1,000 worth of time to save $5 is not making wise use of any institution's scarce resources.

In procurement and education, there are some rules to keep in mind. An institution typically spends about 25 percent of its budget on goods and services through procurement—a little more if it is highly centralized, a little less if it is not. About 10 percent of the 25 percent can be accomplished using consortium contracts. If more buying is done on contracts, all the better, for this delivers faster results to end users and saves time and money.

Cost Containment

Consortia and purchasing departments help to contain costs and therefore contribute instantly to the bottom line, an idea that is popular with parents, students, taxpayers, presidents, legislators, and trustees. School do fail from time to time, and consolidation is not beyond the realm of possibility. Every time a school fails, the options of choice are reduced to students. The goal of consortia has to be helping members to contain costs as they carry out their mission of teaching, research, and community service.

The Massachusetts Higher Education Consortium

The Massachusetts Higher Education Consortium (MHEC) is a twenty-four-year-old public purchasing consortium with thirty-four public and fifty private members. It was the first to join together public and private, sectarian and nonsectarian schools under one membership. When it was formed as a public purchasing consortium as the result of a governor's management task force, the founding committee consulted with the Massachusetts Attorney General's Office. An attorney general, the head of the state's Contracts Division, had the imagination and foresight to see that the joining together of public and private, big and small, for the common good and mission would be good for Massachusetts. Ground rules were established concerning contracting in the public sector through sealed bids, but private institutions were allowed to join and bring their purchasing volume to the mix.

Some consortia operate by retaining a percentage of the discounts offered by vendors. Others, such as the MHEC, collect dues from the member schools, giving the members the full benefit of lower prices or higher discounts. Dues are tied to the school's last three-year average of purchased volume. Small schools that buy less pay less in dues, and big schools that buy more pay more. The dues levels from minimum to maximum are tied to the MHEC's total operating budget.

In 1998, the MHEC was formally recognized under the Massachusetts General Law. This allowed the field of membership to expand to "any higher education institution within the Commonwealth." The original field of membership had been defined by the attorney general as "any private school that is tied to a state school through a formal bond, such as, incorporation of an academic consortium." For many years, the membership remained constant at fifty-seven, but after the law passed, the membership grew steadily to eighty-four. It is a 501(c)(3) tax-exempt association. The MHEC receives no appropriation or taxpayer money, owns all its own equipment, is debt free, and pays all its own operating expenses. The University of Massachusetts at Amherst has always provided space and other services, for which the MHEC waives the Amherst campus dues.

In its first full year of operation, the member schools used MHEC contracts to obtain $1.5 million in goods and services. In fiscal year 2001, the membership did a volume of $153.5 million.

The MHEC has eighty-two contracts in place with about six hundred vendors, with contracts ranging from computers to caps and gowns, from lab supplies to lawn mowers, from furniture to facilities maintenance materials. There is no member school that does not use some vendor. Annual volumes range from $15.8 million for the largest user down to $26,000 for the newest member. In 2001 three schools did over $10 million in volume, forty-one did over $1 million, twenty-five did between $500,000 and $1 million, and seventeen more did between $100,000 and $500,000. Thirty-six vendors did over $1 million in volume.

Purchasing consortia are on the ascendancy, not decline, as more and more schools feel the budget pinch and try to do more with less. The MHEC grew 32 percent in 2001 on top of 22 percent in 2000. To ignore taking advantage of consortium contracting as a valuable tool for educational institutions is to miss an important opportunity. Downsized purchasing departments in institutions where end users are now empowered to do more and more of the routine buying need to provide their campuses with a tool box that contains more contracts. To create and manage those contracts school by school does not make as much sense as a group of schools working on contracting together.

How to Get Started

Usually, a group of schools within close proximity will get together to discuss issues and needs of common interest. The group may also be related, such as all the community colleges within one state or all the Catholic schools in one area.

It is highly unlikely that any group of schools will have the luxury of a budget with which to form a staffed consortium. On the other hand, trustees or the college presidents may mandate more cooperation and the sharing of expertise and resources.

Often a group of schools may elect to create a common contract for goods or a service. A committee or a lead purchasing agent may create the contract specification to bid such a joint contract. The contract could be for one common item such as fuel or fertilizer, or it may cover a complete category such as lab supplies or dormitory furniture. In the beginning, it is likely that there will be no budget to support such a cooperative effort, so it will be handled by volunteers sharing the workload.

Consortium groups will have more success if they use standard terms and conditions on formal request for bid forms. Each member will have terms and conditions that it has been using. If the committee or a lead agent goes through all the variations in terms, it can borrow the best from each and create standard terms and conditions for the group-buying consortium to use. This will bring consistency and continuity to the process, which will give confidence to bidders. If bidders do not have to pad their bids to protect themselves from the unknown and unforeseen, their bids will be stronger.

If the terms and conditions are saved on computer, they can be used and modified on future bids, streamlining the creation process. Over time, bidders will come to understand how the consortium operates. They see that the conditions for contracting are clear and spelled out, and that gives them confidence that the consortium is not making up the rules as it goes along.

Today, working with vendors is a partnership; therefore, it is important that the purchasing group project an air of honesty, firmness, and fairness. Bidding should have the goal of producing more bids, not fewer, so the process should encourage response. Never should a bidder throw bids away because of being been burned by a buyer and no longer trusting the process.

If the specifications include a provision for the group to retain a small percentage of any discount, after a time this will create a fund that will help offset operating expenses. If the schools can realize and document savings or cost avoidance, they may elect to create a dues structure to support the consortium. There will be expenses—printing, postage, forms, and letterhead, for example—and no single member may be willing to absorb this expense on behalf of all members.

Some purchasing groups start by choosing to share responsibility. A purchasing agent who is very knowledgeable about furniture may volunteer to handle the furniture contract. Another may handle lab supplies, another the contract for paper or office supplies.

The biggest roadblock to cooperation may prove to be turf and ego. Member agents must agree at the outset to cooperate, share, participate, and benefit. Participation may be more acceptable if the group elects to make use of any contract optional and not try to force committed volume contracts, where all must commit to their fair share. They may need to compromise on specifications or brands for the common good. A multivendor, multibrand contract will help a group get over this hurdle.

There have been cases where a group came together only to learn that some of the members already have a good contract in place. School A may have a very good lab supply contract, School B a good office supply contract, School C a contract with travel agents, and so on. The solution can be as simple as each asking its vendor whether it would be willing to extend the benefits of the contract to more schools (customers). Rarely will a vendor turn its back on potential business and refuse. Consequently, a group of schools will have created an instant purchasing consortium. If this arrangement is successful and members can see that they are saving time and money, they may be encouraged to try a new joint contract that none of the schools has enjoyed previously. Success will breed success if members are allowed and encouraged to be creative as they innovate beyond their prior experience.

Group purchasing produces instant, measurable results that go immediately to a school's bottom line. An institution that saves $100 on a product or service has instantly freed up $100 of a finite budget to be used elsewhere. Buying from an established contract also streamlines the administrative process, freeing people to move on to other worthwhile projects where they can add real value. A purchasing consortium creates a win-win-win program that will be popular with all constituents: vendors, end users, and tuition-paying students and parents. Furthermore, improving the process also extends to vendors, which benefit from not having to answer numerous quotes and bids. Vendors that are saving time and money while accessing new and expanded opportunities will pass on improved discounts and pricing.

For a group purchasing consortium to produce contracts and save institutions time and money is only half of the equation. If a consortium writes into its bid terms that successful vendors must report back to the consortium the volume of business done with each member on each contract, they will do that. Armed with these data, the consortium should prepare an annual report that documents what has been accomplished and what has been saved or costs avoided. It may also document meetings, member-vendor product expo shows, the volume done by vendors, and the total volume done on each contract.

If the consortium reaches a point where it is collecting and expending funds, those accounts should be audited, and a financial report should be included in the annual report. This report should be shared though each member institution so the institution will know what has been accomplished by taking advantage of group buying.

Conclusion

It is time for purchasing professionals in higher education to move on to larger concepts and be creative and imaginative. Participation in a consortium provides access to a dedicated service provider that lets members buy more effectively, from reliable sources with lower administrative costs, and with shorter lead times from the inception of need to the delivery of product. The strength of the consortium will depend on the loyalty and unity of the group; the negotiating power will relate directly to the degree of common participation.

JAKE E. BISHOP is chair and chief executive officer of the Massachusetts Higher Education Consortium in Amherst.

11

*International programs are important to developing
sustainable and cost-effective programs that provide
an excellent national model of collaboration among
institutions.*

A Collaborative Approach to
International Programs

Galen C. Godbey, Barbara Turlington

In anticipating the continuation of globalization trends in economic, cultural, and governmental affairs, colleges and universities must make a
deeper commitment to preparing global-ready graduates. Many institutions,
especially small to medium-sized ones, will benefit from agile, collaborative
approaches to both overseas and campus-based activities and programs.
Despite the constraints and entanglements of collaboration, it can provide
the scale and quality of resources that participants needed to sustain cost-
effective, high-quality programs over time.

Globalization

Globalization is arguably the central social, cultural, political, and economic phenomenon of our times. As Tom Friedman argues in *The Lexus
and the Olive Tree* (2000), it can be seen as the successor system to the cold
war system. Work, in both nonprofit and for-profit sectors, is increasingly
geographically distributed, technologically mediated, interorganizational,
team based, problem or project focused, collaborative, multicultural, and
international.

Colleges and universities must plan their futures in the context of a
globalizing world, where not only economic production, but as John
Micklethwait and Adrian Wooldridge (2000) suggest, leisure, social wel-
fare policies, and even the rituals of death are now subject to external influences, commercial and otherwise.

Americans must commit to mastering the art of global organization for
reasons cultural, political, economic, and, most certainly, demographic. As

New Directions for Higher Education, no. 120, Winter 2002 © Wiley Periodicals, Inc.

the U.S. population shrinks as a percentage of the world's total, the agility and global sophistication of American workers will be crucial determinants of our capacity to maintain our institutions and influence. By 2030, the population ratio of people living in industrialized or developed nations compared to those living in developing nations will be one to four; as recently as 1995, this ratio was one to two (Lutz, 1994). Given these powerful probabilities, the fact that U.S. colleges and universities send only 3 percent of their students on study-abroad programs borders on scandal.

Moreover, despite the fact that English is currently the dominant language of the Internet and of international business, to the point that some critics of globalization use that term interchangeably with *Americanization,* it should be noted that the percentage of the world's population that speaks English as a primary language is decreasing. Only 7.6 percent of the world's population speaks English as its native tongue, and only 20 percent speak a Western language of any type as a native language (Huntington, 1996). The combination of poverty, limited schooling, cultural inertia and chauvinism, and explosive birth rates in so-called developing countries could keep English an elite language, barring major social, political, and economic changes in these struggling nations.

At the other end of the spectrum, recent decisions by the leaders of European universities promise tremendous opportunities for both increased collaboration and competition between American and European institutions. Under pressure from the European Union, which is encouraging academic and labor mobility within Europe through a variety of means, most university leaders have promised to adopt a common model for undergraduate and first-level graduate degrees. At present, the first degree is awarded after three years in the United Kingdom, whereas until recently in Germany and Italy, four to seven years might be required for the first degree, usually the equivalent of a master's degree in the United States. Within the next five to seven years, most European institutions are expected to embrace an American-style progression from bachelor's degree followed by a master's degree. Assuming the continuation of affordable air travel and declining telecommunications rates, these more similar formats will greatly advance the integration of the United States and Western European educational programs and intellectual resources—an academic analogue to the economic integration that has taken place in the recent past. Small to medium-sized American colleges and universities may need to form consortia in order to partner effectively with European and other foreign universities, which tend to be larger and have had little experience with American-style liberal arts colleges or community colleges.

Globalization, Agility, and Higher Education

A fundamental assumption is that the processes by which people are educated need to be broadly consistent with the way in which organizations operate in a globalizing environment. It is not enough for schools and colleges to deliver content aimed at preparing students for global involvement or to send students abroad for a semester or year, as valuable and necessary as these experiences are. Students and faculty must learn and work in ways that model the globalizing reality of organizational behavior.

The creation of mass higher education and the Carnegie Unit in the 1950s and 1960s was consistent with the norms and needs of the period: mass production for largely undifferentiated domestic markets, conscripted mass armies, and mass media (both print and television). Education must now be restructured and reanimated for a world of mass customization, agility, and routine international interaction, whether the interaction serves cultural, intellectual, commercial, or religious goals. Graduates need to be able to move seamlessly into globally oriented organizations and feel at home in that model.

To function successfully in a globalizing world, organizations need to increase their agility. Agile organizations are fast, flexible, collaborative, and customizing. They have moved beyond stand-alone models of staff behavior and organizational relationships to internal and external collaboration, usually mediated by technology, as a first-choice strategy.

In collaborative approaches to internationalizing education, the traditional loose coupling of faculty and staff is unsustainable: collaboration within institutions, as well as across institutions, is essential for internationalizing and globalizing educational programs and other areas of institutional development. One of the worst things that can befall an institution in an environment that values or assumes cooperative solutions is to be seen as an incompetent or unreliable partner.

Examples of Consortial Strategies and Programs

Increasing awareness of the need for internationalizing programs in all fields and disciplines has led to increased awareness of the need for collaboration to meet this imperative. The following examples of consortia involved in international education and international development projects are just a few of the growing number of collaborative efforts in this area.

Some academic consortia have existed for decades, with multiple areas of collaboration; others are recent and may be focused on international collaboration for the long term; still others may be responding to a particular short-term problem or opportunity. Some concentrate on joint curricular projects and some on increasing opportunities for students to study abroad. Many involve only U.S. institutions, but an increasing number include universities from two or three countries working together. Some are initiated and funded by government agencies in the United States and in other countries or regions; others are funded primarily or entirely by the collaborating institutions.

Major differences exist in the staffing of these groups. Some, like most of those put together in response to the programs offered by funding agencies, have no permanent staff and rely on the work of a few committed faculty members; others, especially the multipurpose consortia that have a long history, have developed extensive permanent staffs. Those with permanent staffs have a better chance of surviving and sustaining their international efforts because the staff can spend time in supporting faculty efforts and raising outside funds and because staffing supported by institutional membership fees and internal funding implies a level of institutional commitment to the joint endeavor. Some of the consortia started for a single purpose, such as library cooperation or building a collaborative program with a single institution abroad, have grown and prospered beyond the initial funding.

Community of Agile Partners in Education (CAPE) is an example of a long-standing multiple-purpose consortium. CAPE (www.acape.org) is a 501(c)(3) nonprofit consortium of over one hundred Pennsylvania colleges, universities, school districts, and other organizations using technology to promote educational cooperation and resource sharing. One program that CAPE has supported is Integrated Product Development (IPD) teams, a multi- and interdisciplinary team-based approach to learning that focuses on the entrepreneurial process of developing actual products. Student teams, with faculty and industrial mentors, design and prepare prototypes of products to solve real-world problems at the request of major corporations and local entrepreneurs. At leading university-based IPD programs, while student teams frequently produce patentable products, it is the student-team experience in bringing a new product to market that truly matters. Employers have been exceptionally pleased with the productivity of students who have participated in IPD programs.

CAPE's involvement with IPD began in 1999 when, as part of a $1.5 million grant from the National Aeronautics and Space Administration, it funded a project with Lehigh University in Bethlehem, Pennsylvania, to internationalize its IPD project. Lehigh linked its student teams through technology with teams from Fontys Technical University in the Netherlands and the Otto-von-Guericke-Universität Magdeburg in Germany. Despite cultural differences and differences in academic processes and incentive systems, this alliance has developed into a regular feature of Lehigh's IPD program. (For more information about IPD as practiced at Lehigh, see www. lehigh.edu/ipd/.) John Ochs, director of Lehigh University's IPD program, reports that students from the humanities and social sciences contribute as much to product design as do students from engineering or business.

Clearly, IPD practitioners and advocates have a major pedagogical story to tell, and one with implications for not only the intellectual cohesiveness and effectiveness of educational institutions, but for national economic competitiveness and international relationships. When students from multiple institutions use technology to facilitate their teamwork, especially when those students represent different countries or cultures, a complex and exceptionally exciting and effective learning environment can be created. Indeed, adding technology, interinstitutional collaboration, and international

dimensions to IPD teams creates a learning experience that directly corre-
lates with the globalized production environments in which more and more
organizations operate.

CAPE now has a well-established, ongoing IPD interest group that
involves representatives of both K–12 and postsecondary institutions who
are devoted to securing external funds to disseminate and implement IPD
within CAPE and with additional international partners.

Another long-standing multipurpose consortium is Five Colleges,
Incorporated in western Massachusetts (www.fivecolleges.edu). Begun in the
1950s with Amherst, Mount Holyoke, and Smith Colleges and the University
of Massachusetts at Amherst, the consortium added the newly formed
Hampshire College as its fifth member in 1969. Its earliest programs were in
shared library resources and joint programs in astronomy and the history of
science. Now students at all five institutions enroll freely (with an adviser's
consent) in courses at the other four, and shared programs include international, area studies, and foreign language programs in Africa, Asia, East Asia,
Latin America, the Middle East, and Canada, as well as in international relations, peace and world security studies, multicultural theater, an East Asian
languages program, and a self-instructional language program. Three area
studies and foreign language centers have received foundation funds or federal funding through the Title VI program of the U.S. Department of
Education but now operate primarily on funds from the five institutions.
Faculty members in these various area studies meet regularly (facilitated by
the consortium staff); collaboration in some cases extends to consultation
on faculty appointments in a variety of disciplines to meet area studies needs
and joint faculty appointments in fields such as peace and world security
studies. Thus, each institution can offer its students a much broader range
of programs than any could offer on its own.

The Five College Center for World Languages (www.umass.edu/fclrc/
fclrc.htm), funded by a grant from the Mellon Foundation, ensures that students at all five institutions have access to the latest teaching and learning
methods and equipment. Technical support and staff consultants help faculty design new course components. The center coordinates the Five
College Self-Instructional Language programs, does video conversions
between different regional video standards for faculty and members of the
community, and publishes a journal in conjunction with the National
Association of Self-Instructional Language Programs. The program has pro-
duced the Five College Foreign Language Laserdisc to support study of the
least commonly taught languages.

Other consortia have been established primarily to foster collaboration
in international programs. For instance, the Global Partners Project, funded
by the Mellon Foundation, is a collaborative effort of three regional associations: the Associated Colleges of the Midwest, the Associated Colleges of the
South, and the Great Lakes Colleges Association. These forty-one liberal arts
colleges collaborate to strengthen their international education programs

through developing cross-consortial connections, thus reducing redundancy and improving quality. Several task forces focus on best practices and effective models for off-campus study, preparation, reentry, and faculty and professional development and on language teaching using effective technology, as well as developing student and faculty programs in Turkey, East Africa, and Central Europe/Russia. (See the project's Web site at www.41colleges.org.)

Several limited-purpose consortia concentrate on the joint development of curriculum by faculty members at more than one institution. For instance, faculty members at Denison College and Kenyon College in Ohio have developed a collaborative program in Middle Eastern, South Asian, and international studies, and distance courses have been developed in introductory Japanese and advanced Chinese. (The Web site at www.enhancedlearning.org/mellon/proj/index.html lists the projects in detail.)

The Birmingham Area Consortium for Higher Education, a group of five public and private colleges and universities, has created the English Language and Culture Institute that will primarily serve the language needs of international students and researchers at the five institutions. The project has three main goals: to meet the English-language learning needs of international students and researchers on the campuses, to meet the English-language needs of the growing international population of the Birmingham area, and to meet the language and cross-cultural training needs of businesses in the area. It recently received a grant of $20,000 from the Community Foundation of Greater Birmingham to aid in this project. (See www.bache.org for more information.)

The U.S. government, through the Fund for the Improvement of Postsecondary Education, supports three collaborative programs: the Program for North American Mobility in Higher Education, the European Community United States of America Cooperation Program in Higher and Vocational Education and Training, and the US-Brazil Higher Education Consortia (see www.ed.gov/offices/OPE/FIPSE/ for detailed information about these programs). All three programs receive funding from both the United States and other participating governments. The North American program requires two universities or colleges in each country to work together on developing curriculum and encouraging student mobility. For instance, the North American Alliance for Sustainable Water Resources brings together Michigan Technological University, New Mexico State University, Université Laval, the University of British Columbia, Universidad de Sonora, and Universidad Veracruzana in a collaborative effort to develop a program of study in sustainable water resource management.

The European Community program requires two U.S. institutions to work with two institutions from different countries in Europe. The US-Brazil Program requires two institutions from each country; it fosters university partnerships through the exchange of undergraduate and graduate students, faculty, and staff within the context of bilateral curricular development.

Students benefit from having an international curriculum and cultural dimension added to their studies through a combination of bilateral curricular innovation and study abroad.

The Liaison Office for University Cooperation in Development (ALO), a group sponsored by six higher education associations and funded by the U.S. Agency for International Development, funds collaborative projects between U.S. institutions of higher education and those in developing countries. (See www.aascu.org/alo/ for more information.)

One example of their projects is a special initiative in Macedonia. Led by Indiana University, the project supports efforts to establish a new private, multilingual, multicultural university in Tetovo, a predominantly ethnic Albanian community in northwest Macedonia. This partnership includes an existing consortium in a collaboration with an international partner; it will draw on the resources and expertise of the Indiana Consortium for International Programs, in particular Indiana University–Bloomington; Ball State University; Butler University; Indiana University–Southeast; and Indiana University–Purdue University, Indianapolis. The partnership is part of an overarching multimillion dollar initiative of the Organization for Security and Cooperation in Europe. The program sponsors expect that the benefits of the program will be not only for Macedonia, but also for the participating U.S. institutions that will be able to provide many international opportunities for their faculty and students.

Some collaborations under the ALO program are specifically designed to help development activities. The Eastern Iowa Community College District and Vasavi College of Engineering work together to develop the educational infrastructure to promote and sustain a community college system in South India. Kapiolani Community College and the Ceylon Hotel School Graduates Association worked to develop the tourism workforce in both Sri Lanka and Hawaii through faculty and student exchanges to promote economic development.

Cornell University, Purdue University, and the Pan American School of Agriculture in Honduras developed an integrated program of education, applied research, and outreach activities to address critical needs in sustainable resource management, human resource development, and economic growth.

The Association Liaison Office has established a Web-based database, CUPID, through which institutions can find partners for collaborative projects.

Whether such collaboratives, established to serve particular purposes and funded by external agencies for a limited number of years, will prove to be sustainable is an open question. Surely most of them will result in increased international awareness and opportunities for faculty development and student exchange on the cooperating campuses. Some of them will result in long-term collaborations among faculty members at the participating institutions in research or in student mobility, but may not lead to additional programs or structures that support long-term cooperation. We believe that the agile institution must be able to take advantage of short-term opportunities and meet short-term challenges, as well as plan on internationalization for the long haul. Some of these projects may answer those needs.

Some collaborative efforts among institutions may not yet qualify as consortia but clearly enhance international opportunities for students and may develop into more formal structures. For instance, a number of partnerships have been formed to develop joint programs or to offer courses on-line. The University of Guanajuato in Mexico and Southern Oregon University are offering a joint master's degree in management. San Diego State University offers a joint program in business with a Mexican university through which students do two years at each university and receive a degree from each. Western Illinois University has formed a consortium to offer a joint master's degree in business administration program with the University of Ottawa and the Autonomous University of Queretaro; students will complete a semester at each institution and a research or internship project in one of the three countries.

Princeton University and the University of Oxford have announced a significant expansion of their academic and research collaboration with a major partnership covering a wide range of disciplines. The program will include the humanities, social sciences, engineering, mathematics, and science. They project an increased number of senior academics, graduate students, and undergraduates crossing the Atlantic in both directions, as well as additional joint research projects and sharing of expensive academic resources. "Both institutions see the new program as a way to strengthen their academic stature and to compete in the globalized higher-education environment, with the added bonus of having access to joint funds from international foundations, multinational corporations, the American and British governments, and possibly the European Union. Research and learning increasingly are global endeavors, involving collaboration among faculty members and students from around the world," said Harold T. Shapiro, Princeton's president, in announcing the effort (Birchard, 2002, p. A45). A joint committee identified twelve projects for initial collaboration. Projects for 2001–2002 included aerospace and automotive design, eastern Mediterranean culture and religion, astrophysics, nanotechnology, art preservation, and bioinformatics.

Recognizing the need for cross-cultural competencies in business and the advantages of a division of labor, seventeen European management schools have combined with fifty-five corporate partners to offer a master's degree in international business.

Another international consortium is the Consortium for North American Higher Education Collaboration (CONAHEC; http://conahec. org/), which exists to facilitate collaborative projects among higher education institutions in Canada, Mexico, and the United States. CONAHEC has developed a listserv and a database to help institutions find suitable partners.

Reflections on Effective Strategies

Each of these models of consortia has its strengths and weaknesses. Some of those cited—for instance the ALO-supported collaborations—serve the need for "agility"—the ability of institutions to capture swiftly important opportunities or solve particular problems through flexible, collaborative, and customized responses. They may not be intended to be long-lasting collaborations. Others, which may be funded for only three or four years, are founded with the hope that they will be sustainable over time, with the lessons learned during the period of building trust among faculty members from several institutions and during initial exchanges of faculty and students leading to sustained collaborative relationships. The question about such efforts is whether it is possible to sustain these relationships without a structure of collaboration, including committed funding, permanent staff, and related activities that will build on the often rather fragile beginnings.

With an ongoing long-term consortium like Five Colleges, the structure, staffing, and financial commitments can be used to sustain programs. These take a large amount of effort and time.

Making Collaboration in International Education Work

Wayne Anderson (1999), president of the Associated Colleges of the South, offers important advice to consortia about to embark on a collaborative international program:

- Earn, get, and keep strong support from Presidents and Provosts.
- Identify key faculty at each participating institution who will passionately promote participation in the program.
- Be sure that institutions are whole-heartedly committed to a multiyear test of program feasibility—don't pressure reluctant institutions into joining the effort.
- Document the academic value added by the programs, and use satisfied students in your marketing.
- Plan methodically, even if it means a later starting date for your project or program—once you've developed confidence in the consortial approach, additional activities may be undertaken with greater speed.
- Make sure all parties understand how decisions regarding the purposes, structure, operation, evaluation, and future of the program or project will be made.

- Make sure that participating individuals and institutions are properly insured.
- Be prepared to terminate unsuccessful programs if they fail to meet their stated goals.
- Make sure that the consortium or institution charged with administering the program can commit necessary staff resources: inadequate staffing and funding can lead to embarrassment for all.

While most of these points are administrative commonplaces, the consortial and international nature of the enterprise raises the stakes. More than one intercultural project has foundered on assumptions that consensus had been achieved and that all parties were prepared for long-term investments: polite conversations and handshakes are no substitutes for clear understanding and written agreements.

Conclusion

The programs we have described prove both the viability and significant benefits of well-planned collaboration in the globalization of higher education. In the emerging global organizational environment for education, the importance of relationship capital—the educational, strategic, and developmental power of trust relationships—can only grow. The day of the stand-alone institution in international education, as in so many other spheres, is over.

References

Anderson, W. "Cooperating Internationally." In L. Dotolo and J. T. Strandness (eds.), *Best Practices in Higher Education Consortia: How Institutions Can Work Together.* New Directions in Higher Education, no. 106. San Francisco: Jossey-Bass, 1999.

Birchard, K. *Chronicle of Higher Education,* Feb. 12, 2002, 47(34), A45.

Friedman, T. *The Lexus and the Olive Tree.* New York: Farrar Straus & Giroux, 2000.

Huntington, S. *The Clash of Civilizations and the Remaking of the World Order.* New York: Simon & Schuster, 1996.

Lutz, W. "The Future of World Population." *Population Bulletin,* 1994, 49(1), 28.

Micklethwaite, J., and Wooldridge, A. *Future Perfect.* New York: Crown Business Books, 2000.

GALEN C. GODBEY *is the executive director of a Community of Agile Partners in Education in Bethlehem, Pennsylvania.*

BARBARA TURLINGTON *is director of international education for the American Council on Education in Washington, D.C.*

12

Consortia can use television to serve the educational needs of the community and at the same time form strategic alliances with other agencies to enhance their efforts to meet the demands of their clientele.

Cooperation and Alliances: Higher Education and the Use of Television

Lawrence G. Dotolo

The Virginia Tidewater Consortium for Higher Education, a consortium of fifteen colleges and universities located in the Hampton Roads area of Virginia, has operated its own cable television channel for the past twenty-one years. This channel has provided the citizens in the Hampton Roads area with higher education programming, including college credit classes. What is important in the establishment and operation of the consortium's Higher Education Cable Channel is not only what is offered but what is presented to the public in terms of information about the colleges.

How the Television Effort Began

The interest in using television as a medium for education existed almost from the beginning of the medium. In the late 1950s and early 1960s, the colleges and universities in the United States expressed great interest in delivering college courses for credit, the most famous of these being New York University's Sunrise Semester. These courses were little more than talking heads, but they were popular with the viewing audience and lasted for almost a decade. The courses did prove that people would enroll in classes for college credit on television. Later, when the Public Broadcasting System (PBS) became interested in developing high-quality courses, such as *Adam's Chronicles* and *The Ascent of Man*, there emerged a greater interest in offering college courses on television.

The Virginia Tidewater Consortium for Higher Education became involved in television courses (telecourses) at that time. From the very beginning of this endeavor in the late 1970s and early 1980s, the colleges

New Directions for Higher Education, no. 120, Winter 2002 © Wiley Periodicals, Inc.

and universities of the consortium saw this as a cooperative project because of the considerable expense involved. Because the telecourses were new, the colleges were not sure how well they would do in terms of enrollment. Thus, they thought that sharing the marketing expenses made excellent sense. Because the courses were of such a high quality and widely advertised, they were very successful, with enrollments in the hundreds. The difficulty, which arose from this success, was that the colleges wanted to offer more courses, but there was very little courseware available with the exception of courses from Dallas Community College, the Great Plains Network, and other similar places. The problem with these courses was the expense of purchasing licensing rights and enrollment fees. For many of the colleges and universities, the costs were prohibitive and a disincentive for colleges that wanted to expand their method of delivering college courses.

It was the onset of the PBS Adult Learning Service that gave the colleges and universities the opportunity to participate in televised college courses at a greatly reduced rate. Colleges and universities now had the opportunity to access a large number of courses at a relatively low cost. The PBS efforts through the Adult Learning Service to form active partnerships with colleges and universities and consortia of institutions were the keys to enhancing the use of college telecourses. In essence, these telecourses became the first significant nationwide distance-education attempt by colleges and universities since the beginning of correspondence courses. The increase in the number of telecourses and the great interest from the public in these courses presented the colleges with an interesting dilemma: the demand outpaced their ability to deliver. In the area of Virginia served by the Consortium for Higher Education, the options were very limited.

The Beginning of the Partnerships

The consortium formed a partnership with the local PBS station, WHRO Telecommunications Center, to air some of the telecourses on its open-air channel. However, WHRO had only limited times available because it was established to deliver primarily to K–12 education. Thus, the consortium had to search elsewhere for access if it intended to offer courses in significant number. It opted to meet with Cox Cable with the intention of asking Cox for a few hours on its public access channel. Cox, however, perceived the consortium's colleges working together as an entity as extremely important, and it wanted to form a partnership in order to enhance its public image, which had become tarnished over franchise battles with the local jurisdictions. What surprised the consortium was Cox's eagerness for the consortium to have its own channel on its system. Cox wanted the consortium to schedule programs at least twelve hours per day, and it was willing to provide some of the equipment.

In order for the consortium to accept Cox's generous offer, it had to look to one of its own members to be the origination point for access to the

Cox system. Tidewater Community College volunteered to be that point; it agreed to staff the project and provide the needed equipment without charge to the consortium members. This effort gave the other colleges the opportunity to offer a significant number of college telecourses and to have access to a dedicated channel for higher education on a major cable system. When the consortium entered into a partnership with Cox Cable, they were serving only three cities in the Hampton Roads area: Norfolk, Portsmouth, and Virginia Beach. Thus, the consortium had to form agreements with other cable companies. This process was slow, since many of the other companies (unlike Cox) did not want to give up their channel space for higher education.

The process to expand the reach of the consortium's Higher Education Cable Channel was involved and complicated. Because of the geography of the region, mainly the Chesapeake Bay, the consortium had to find a different place for the origination of the Higher Education Cable Channel because a low-power microwave signal was needed to reach the towers of other cable companies. This low-power microwave, known as Instructional Television Fixed System (ITFS), was licensed to WHRO television, the local PBS station. Thus, the consortium's board of directors decided to enter into a partnership with WHRO to allow it to be the technical operating center for the Higher Education Cable Channel. The consortium was required to pay a fee to WHRO for this service, a fee that was a fraction of the cost of the true operational expense. This partnership with WHRO proved to be fortuitous because it gave the consortium the potential to expand the channel to reach outlying areas and the opportunity to have a professional-looking channel that operated twenty-fours a day, seven days a week. With WHRO's satellite capabilities, the consortium was able to receive programs from a variety of sources that could provide programming resources for its channel.

The ability to reach other cable companies gave the consortium the option to form partnerships with cable companies interested in having a higher education channel that had consistent and quality programming twenty-four hours a day. What has hurt many cable companies over the years are public access channels that go unused or are underused. Thus, many cable companies are reluctant to give up space to public entities that cannot provide the necessary programming. Because the consortium, through its partnership with WHRO, had access to programming, it was able to form partnership agreements with other cable companies. These agreements allow the consortium to enhance its cable penetration greatly and expand its influence in the Hampton Roads community.

The partnership between the consortium and Cox Cable is unique. Cox deals only with the consortium and not with the individual institutions that are consortium members. From Cox's standpoint, this makes perfect sense since it does not have to deal with fifteen individual institutions that may have wanted to have their own cable access channel. The colleges and the universities of the consortium recognized early that using television for the delivery of college courses and other informational programming was expensive and best accomplished as a consortium. WHRO has essentially adopted the same philosophy that it would rather deal with the consortium than with a multitude of institutions. Both Cox and WHRO have kept the agreements simple and the arrangements straightforward. There is no positioning, no institution angling to improve its individual situation. This results in programs that are good for all institutions, not just a few.

The importance of partnerships in the use of television is evident. No one institution could sustain the tremendous effort it requires to maintain a full-time cable channel. The sharing of the costs allows institutions to do more because of the economies of scale. The value of a full-time higher education cable channel is incalculable to the colleges and universities; to the cable company, it is approximately $1 million a year in revenue lost that it would have received from advertisers. Thus, the consortium and its partners realize the operational and public relations value of having such a resource for this unencumbered use. This freedom to expand and form other relationships has given the consortium the opportunity to create programming and establish partnerships with non–higher education entities.

External Partnerships

The consortium's effort to form relationships with the various constituencies in the community was an important factor that allowed the significant Hispanic community in the Hampton Roads area to have its own Spanish television programming. The consortium offered through its satellite reception of foreign news broadcast Spanish news as well as news from other countries throughout the world. Eventually, because of the success of the foreign news broadcasts, Cox Cable opted to offer a full-time Spanish-language channel. The consortium's early response to the interest in a Spanish news channel was a significant help to Cox Cable in that it allowed it the time to build channel capacity before adding a full-time Spanish channel. Cox was grateful for the consortium's help in alleviating what could have been a serious public relations problem for it.

The consortium, because of the valuable asset of the Higher Education Cable Channel, has been able to establish positive relationships with agencies outside higher education. The Norfolk Public School System wanted to have its weekly program shown on the Higher Education Cable Channel because so many of its teachers live outside Norfolk and were not able to view the informational programs. This special relationship with the public schools has aided the consortium in forming other programs dealing with teachers and students, and in some cases the consortium and the Norfolk Public School System have submitted joint proposals to the U.S. Department of Education and private foundations.

There are other examples of forming partnerships that do not directly benefit the consortium but are of tremendous benefit to the community.

One of these is with the Virginia Beach Fire Department, which wanted to offer in-service programs to firefighters and emergency service personnel on duty at their local firehouses. The Virginia Beach Fire Department is offering the televised training programs to all the emergency and fire department personnel in the Hampton Roads area. Thus, the consortium's Higher Education Cable Channel was one of the few options available to the Fire Department. The consortium views the offering of these programs as a public service and a means of positioning it to provide educational services to emergency personnel when the need arises.

The Public Relations Value of Television Access

The most important strategic move that the consortium has made was to establish a monthly television program, *Inside Higher Education in Hampton Roads*. The program follows a talk show format, where topics germane to higher education are discussed. The value of the program lies in the fact that the consortium can offer agencies that may be tangentially related to higher education television time that they could not afford to purchase on commercial television. The consortium recently formed an agreement with an agency involved in workforce development to discuss its efforts to enhance the workforce in the Hampton Roads area. The agreement has led the consortium to form contracts with this agency to perform services related to educating the workforce. The agency is extremely pleased because it is able to receive publicity for its programs over a sustained period of time. The consortium airs its talk program a number of times a week, thus giving maximum exposure to the agency.

The consortium has found that *Inside Higher Education in Hampton Roads* is a perfect vehicle to invite other agencies to discuss their purposes and to place the consortium in position to respond to educational requests by these agencies. Through this effort, the consortium has partnered with other state agencies, such as the Virginia Department of Alcoholic Beverage Control and the State Council for Higher Education in Virginia. Both agencies are important to higher education, and each allowed the consortium the opportunity to focus on issues key to the colleges and the universities. With the Alcohol and Beverage Commission, the consortium focused on alcohol abuse on college campuses, and with the State Council for Higher Education, it gave the council the opportunity to explain its programs and efforts to guide higher education in the state.

Internal Partnerships

Alliances and partnerships relate to more than external organizations; many subsets within the colleges and universities want to partner with the consortium through the use of television. *Inside Higher Education in Hampton Roads,* for example, is an excellent way for these organizations to get their message out to their external constituencies. Many organizations within an institution of higher education have as their primary focus attracting individuals from the community to participate in their programs or who need the services offered by these institutional subsets. One of the members of the Virginia Tidewater Consortium has developed a sophisticated program to recruit personnel separating from the military to become teachers. This effort has been very successful, but there is always the need to present the information to an audience (the military), and that is why a partnership with the consortium made sense. The consortium's wide viewing audience, some 450,000 homes, of which a large number are military, and the ability to show the programs multiple times, made *Inside Higher Education in Hampton Roads* attractive. From the point of view of the consortium, which has counselors working on the bases in the area, promoting one particular program from one university is important for the consortium because it attracts the military client to the services of the colleges through the consortium office.

Another partnership that has developed because of the television capability has been the formation of the International Programs Committee among the colleges and universities, which uses the Higher Education Cable Channel to promote the colleges' and universities' study-abroad programs and international education. This aspect of using television to enhance programs can be an immensely important factor in the relationship between the communities and the colleges and between the consortium and the institutions. The potential for a myriad of partnerships exists. Some may be for a particular event; others could lead to long-term programs. The results, however, can be beneficial to all those involved in the partnership.

Partnerships and alliances are formed for various reasons, and certainly many of them are formed to make the organization more competitive. The consortium, when it first entered into the use of television as a method of delivering college courses, never anticipated the great public relations value that access to a large metropolitan cable system could have for the consortium and its member institutions. Although the original purpose of providing college telecourses is still the main effort, the public relations aspect has quickly become an important factor in the overall plan for the activities of the consortium. The ability to interact with other agencies for the purpose of promoting their programs related to higher education has been immensely valuable and the key to further program development.

Lessons Learned

There are many important lessons learned by the Virginia Tidewater Consortium through its television effort. First, colleges and universities interested in the use of television for offering college courses or for public relations purposes will be surprised by the reaction of both external and internal agencies to the impact of television. Many external agencies are eager to form relations with higher education, and they often see their own programs as having some kind of educational component. There are many organizations in communities that would make excellent partners and may even bring the institution or institutions closer to the surrounding community and more responsive to their needs. For a consortium, the ability to be exposed to a multitude of agencies increases the opportunity of higher education to have a greater impact. Although probably not the only way, having access to cable television in a community, and preferably a dedicated channel like the one the Virginia Tidewater Consortium has, makes higher education a focal point for the community.

An institution or consortium should not limit its energies to establishing alliances and partnerships to external audiences. Through television access, many alliances can be strengthened. These partners may be specifically designed to work with an external population but have not been totally successful because the general public does not know of their existence. Many programs at institutions of higher education languish in relative obscurity because of a lack of public access. In addition, higher education in general has not been particularly good at making its case to the public about its importance and its impact. A continuing presence on television by higher education can produce significant results: more attention by the public to higher education's effort, more support for higher education in the legislature, and more partnerships being developed internally and externally. The consortium can control its own time on the Higher Education Cable Channel; thus, it can repeat its programs as many times as it wishes. This factor makes the use of television even more valuable to its partners because it allows more airtime for the promotion of programs.

Conclusion

There are many factors to consider when establishing partnerships that use television as the focal point of the relationship. The following are points that institutions or consortia should keep in mind when forming relationships:

- Cooperation is a two-way street; each party should expect something for its effort.
- Even casual relationships between organizations can be valuable.
- Not every partnership is suited for television. Some may deal with controversial issues that may hurt an institution or consortium.
- Interest in television as medium to deliver information should be of paramount importance to the potential partners.
- Whenever possible, open-ended partnerships should be avoided. Because television demands frequently change, there can be different interests that develop, or a major event, for example, the September 11, 2001, terrorist attacks, may change public opinion or interests.

Consortia are in the right place in the evolution of television access through the use of cable; however, only a handful of consortia in the United

States are currently operating television access. This is an unfortunate situation because the technology will be changing soon, and there will be many more local cable channels available because of the digitizing of the cable output. These extra channels could be an invaluable asset to a consortium of colleges and universities. They could be used to offer classes, advertise workshops and on-campus activities (the Virginia Tidewater Consortium advertises campus activities between its programs), and promote higher education partnerships, both internal and external. Television, especially cable television, should become a key component of a consortium's effort to promote its activities and to form partnerships. Although it is certainly possible for a single institution to operate a cable channel dedicated to higher education, cooperative efforts among institutions are the most efficient and effective way for institutions to proceed. The high operational expenses would preclude many institutions from pursuing it alone. Television can offer much to colleges and universities through consortial arrangements, even if it is a partial use of an access channel. It can be the catalyst that allows institutions to expand their public relations effort, demonstrate their academic capabilities, and form partnerships that could have a dramatic impact on programs to both internal and external audiences. Most of all, in the true spirit of a partnership, it can be a great asset to the community at large.

LAWRENCE G. DOTOLO is president of the Virginia Tidewater Consortium for Higher Education and also serves as the executive director of the Association for Consortium Leadership in Norfolk, Virginia.

13

The benefits of cooperation through consortium arrangements extend beyond dollars saved.

Assessing a Consortium's Effectiveness

Lorna M. Peterson

In a 1981 report to the Five Colleges, Incorporated board of directors, E. Jefferson Murphy, the consortium's coordinator, wrote: "To date, the increasing cost of Five College cooperation has represented an add-on to institutional budgets but has been tolerable because the complex benefits to students and faculty have appeared to be far greater than the cost to each institution. The time may come when each institution will have to weigh increasing Five College costs in relation to costs within the institutions" (p. 39). Two years later, he wrote, "The Committee also decided early on that it would be imprudent and possibly destructive to envisage Five College cooperation as a device to retrench and economize in hard times. We felt that retrenchment or reallocation of resources, if required during the 1980s, must be undertaken by each institution separately, while using cooperation to protect or increase quality, sustain vitality, and ensure student access to a broad and diverse curriculum" (Five Colleges, Incorporated, 1981, p. 2). The apparent contradiction between these two statements, only two years apart, demonstrates an ongoing tension in the expectations institutions have for consortia: cost savings versus enrichment.

Over twenty years later, Five Colleges still feels the tension. (The member institutions of Five Colleges, Incorporated are Amherst, Hampshire, Mount Holyoke, and Smith Colleges and the University of Massachusetts at Amherst.) Cooperative arrangements are attractive because we assume that they will save money—that by joining together with other institutions, we can reduce costs, and that by sharing resources, we can have more, and better, for less. The idea of Five College cooperation was born in the post–World War II era, when higher education was expanding at an accelerating pace and individual institutions were barely able to keep up with the rate of growth. The leaders of institutions, like many others at that time, believed that the costs of expansion could be contained through partnerships with other institutions. But successful consortia cost money. The more active a consortium is and the more programs and projects it supports, the greater will be the institutional investment.

Understandably, the member institutions want to know how effective consortia are. What do the institutions receive for their investment? Do consortia actually save dollars? If not, what are the benefits, and, more important, how does one measure those benefits? Are they intangible and not quantifiable? In 1997, desiring to address these questions more fully, the Five College board of directors undertook an outside review of the consortium, much like the reaccreditation reviews the institutions undergo periodically. With the support of a grant from the Kellogg Foundation, the board invited a team of distinguished educators to visit the Five Colleges to help assess the impact that cooperation had on the member institutions and to move them ahead in planning for the future. The consortium spent the preceding year gathering information and writing reports, including a staff self-study and reports from the campuses on the impact of the consortium on each of them. In the fall of 1998, representatives from all five institutional boards of trustees attended a joint meeting to discuss the review and their perspectives on the topic. Five Colleges asked the trustees to pose questions they would like to have addressed. These studies, reports, and discussions raised issues about how to measure the success of cooperative programs and how to assess their impact. Some of the measurements looked at dollars spent and dollars saved. Many more were as concerned with the impact of enrichment programs on the campuses as with their costs. A major challenge, therefore, was to find a way to distinguish between activities that needed to be assessed qualitatively and those that should be assessed quantitatively.

Enrichment

The reports on the impact of cooperation on the member institutions all had one refrain in common: the consortium enriches the lives of individual faculty, staff, and students and the cultural life of the institutions themselves. More, not less, cooperation was consistently advocated. Costs were barely mentioned. Instead, the reports noted again and again the importance of a community of faculty colleagues who pool their resources and share their expertise, who present interesting workshops, seminars and symposia, and who jointly host short- and long-term residencies of distinguished scholars and artists. The reports also frequently cited this larger intellectual community as an aid in the recruitment and retention of prospective faculty and students alike. They all refer to the richness of the curriculum, the variety of courses (over six thousand undergraduate courses are offered by the five institutions), majors, interdisciplinary programs, and the great advantage these represent to students, who can freely and easily take courses on the other campuses.

This highly enthusiastic endorsement of the cooperative enterprise as an important enrichment component to campus life is itself one form of assessment. The inherent value of the consortium in terms of satisfaction to its users is, after all, a necessary first step in assessment. It is, however, a qualitative judgment and one made by those who admittedly make use of and enjoy the benefits of cooperative opportunities. What about those who do not participate, who do not take advantage of any of the offerings, that is, the nonusers? This is a question repeatedly raised in discussing assessment. Who is the consortium benefiting? For instance, the number of Five Colleges cross-registrations ranges between forty-two hundred and forty-five hundred annually. Some twenty-five thousand undergraduates are enrolled at the five campuses. Is approximately 20 percent participation sufficient? If not, how do we encourage more? There are two Five Colleges departments and six certificate programs, similar to a minor. The number of students who major in or fulfill the certificate program requirements varies from program to program, from institution to institution, and from year to year. Should there be a threshold of participation to ensure continued support? If so, how does one determine that threshold? Is the user count irrelevant? Is the quality of education available to all students, even if enjoyed by 10 or 20 percent, justification enough? On the other hand, if the consortium did not offer these programs, would there be pressure on the institutions to do so, and what would those costs entail?

There are about two thousand faculty members at the five institutions. More than four hundred a year are members of Five College faculty seminars. Several hundred more are members of Five College councils, committees, programs, and departments. Each year, between twenty and forty teach courses on another campus through faculty exchange agreements. A large number of faculty members from the four undergraduate colleges hold adjunct appointments in the University of Massachusetts graduate school and serve on master's and doctoral committees. The graduate program in history is a University of Massachusetts/Five College program at both the master's and doctoral levels. Members of the history departments at the colleges serve on doctoral committees and advise graduate students; they frequently teach in the graduate program in exchange for university faculty teaching in the undergraduate program. When requesting the creation of a cooperative graduate program, the history faculty argued that it would help attract a larger, more interesting, and more diverse pool of graduate students. When the program comes up for review, that will be one way to measure its success.

But what about the departments and individual faculty who are not engaged in collaborative activities of any kind and do not encourage their students to do so? Faculty and students alike often point to the inconvenience of traveling from campus to campus. (The five campuses are within a ten-mile radius, and there is a fare-free bus system connecting all five.) A recent survey of the Five College transportation system confirmed that in the majority of cases, it requires no more than three course periods to take one course on another campus. Nevertheless, scheduling courses on another campus is a serious logistical problem. Bus schedules alone cannot bridge the miles between the campuses or shorten the time it takes to travel from one campus to another.

Time is an issue for faculty too. Cooperation takes time and energy; it has to be made worthwhile, especially because it is often voluntary on the part of the faculty. At a minimum, the faculty members ask that formal recognition of their participation be instituted in personal evaluations and merit considerations. Some faculty members, however, are resistant for reasons other than time and energy. They believe in the integrity of their own department's curriculum and do not want to interfere with it by collaborating; they do not sufficiently respect programs on other campuses, or they are unwilling to compromise enrollments in their own courses. If increased participation in consortium activities becomes a measure of success, these issues must be addressed, and other obstacles to cooperation will have to be identified.

Should the degree of participation by faculty be the sole measure of success, however? If so, what is the threshold to be sought? More important, how does one measure the value of ongoing cooperative programs, most of which are often add-ons, that is, programs that no one institution could afford to support on its own? Is the value added worth the cost? Can the answer be quantified? Should it be?

In 1998, the Five College Dance Department celebrated its twentieth anniversary. As part of the festivities, the department invited alumni from all five schools back to the campuses for a weekend of performances and workshops. Both faculty and alumni credited the success of the department and its graduates to the strength of the cooperative arrangement, to the number of professors, courses, and dance methods offered—all within a liberal arts context. The alumni publicly attributed their individual achievements to the diversity and balance that a coordinated curriculum ensures.

Clearly, the ability to offer more at less cost continues to be a major value of cooperative programs. When, as is true of the dance department, growth and change take into consideration the needs of the whole department rather than one particular institutional program, it is possible to offer a much broader curriculum. It is also true that the pressure to hire a specialist on each campus in all areas of the field is reduced, particularly if complementarity of offerings is both goal and policy.

Complementarity of Offerings

A major reason for the founding of Five Colleges, Incorporated and other consortia over the past half-century has been the growing need to expand the curriculum. Today, the curriculum is expanding at an even more accelerated rate than before, largely in response to demands for a more international perspective, new discoveries in the sciences, and the impact of computer technology. Interdisciplinary and area studies programs are vying with the needs of more traditional departments and disciplines. The disciplines themselves are expanding beyond the offerings of twenty or thirty years ago. No single curriculum, even at most large universities, can afford to satisfy these competing demands and remain financially viable. By building an interdependent and collaborative curriculum that takes advantage of the strengths of each institution, it is possible to offer more courses, more majors, and more concentrations. A cooperative academic program will be able to provide the advantages of greater depth and range only if all parties agree that personnel decisions will take into consideration the expertise and specializations already available.

Complementarity of offerings can also play a key role in institutional and departmental planning. Sometimes the decision to add—or eliminate—a program can be aided by looking beyond the institution and to the consortium. Several years ago, the pressure to offer the study of Korean within the Five Colleges led to one institution's agreeing to do so with the understanding that it would be the focus campus for Korean and the other institutions would not add Korean to their curricular offerings. Similarly, the burden of eliminating a language or subject from the curriculum of one institution is less problematic if the other institutions agree to continue offering the language on their campuses. Complementarity can also serve departments. For several decades, the Five College philosophy departments have informally, but very successfully, based their faculty searches on consortium-wide needs in the curriculum. They build their individual majors on the assumption that students can and will take advantage of the expertise of faculty on the other campuses. One measure of the consortium's effectiveness is therefore the degree of complementarity among the institutional departments and the flexibility that this affords the institutions in planning for new positions and replacements.

Cost Savings

In some ways, cost savings are far easier to measure than to accomplish. On the whole, joint programs do not save money; rather, they are add-ons that are program enhancing. Institutional budgets, if affected at all, are increased, not reduced. A number of exceptions are worth noting, however, and probably many more are worth seeking. In general, actual dollar savings through consortia are easier to accomplish within administrative areas than within the academic arena. The most obvious and most frequently cited savings come from joint purchasing agreements—for supplies, equipment, and services.

In the past decade, new cooperative programs have been established by Five Colleges and by other consortia that do, in fact, save money for member institutions, actually reducing expenditures. The Five College risk manager and the Five College recycling coordinator are both relatively recent positions and add-ons to the budget. Nevertheless, the expertise they bring to their work saves the institutions more than their positions have cost. In the case of the risk manager, one institution was able to cut a full position. The risk manager uses her knowledge of the insurance industry to solicit joint bids for various policies, thereby saving money for each institution and bringing them better coverage. Similarly, the recycling coordinator has directly saved the four colleges (the University of Massachusetts has its own recycling office and its own office for risk management) costs by bidding jointly for recycling materials, as well as indirectly by increasing the amount of recyclable material they collect. Moreover, the benefits to the entire community are measured more appropriately in years than in dollars. Largely as a result of the collaborative recycling program, the town of Amherst landfill was able to stay active at least five years longer than originally predicted.

Cost Containment

If most consortium programs do not reduce actual expenditures, they often do help to contain costs, particularly the unavoidable costs mandated by changing needs and new demands on the institutions. One of the best Five College examples of cost containment can be found in the extensive cooperation among libraries, which predates the consortium itself. Without repeating the advantages of library cooperation more fully discussed in Chapter Eight, it is worth noting that the foresight of the Five College librarians in the late 1970s resulted in a collaborative effort to share the costs and benefits of an on-line automated library system. At the time, it was a daring move and one that has had positive reverberations ever since. The total dollar investment for the Five College Automated Library System was substantial, yet it was insignificant in comparison to the benefits still accruing and to the total cost if each institution were to have proceeded alone and at its own pace. First, the costs for the hardware and software were largely grant funded because of the uniqueness of the project at that time. Second, costs that were charged to the institutions were far below what would have been the case if any one institution had ventured to automate on its own. Finally, the decision to create a collaborative library system over twenty years ago has inspired more and more cooperation among the libraries, so that today the unavoidable incremental costs to the libraries continue to be contained through joint purchasing, leasing, and training.

A more recent example of how cooperative programs can help contain costs is management training programs, now a common and successful activity for many consortia. The Five College Management Training Collaborative began in response to a strongly felt need on all the campuses to train supervisory personnel and midlevel managers, many of whom had been promoted from the faculty ranks without any training or experience as managers. This occurred at a time when morale was low because of staff reductions or threats of reductions. By working in consort, the schools were able to contain the costs of the program and increase management effectiveness. Management trainers from the campuses form a pool of internal professional consultants from which to draw expertise; when external consultants are needed, their fees are shared, cutting the costs to the institutions. Moreover, here as in other cooperative settings, academic and administrative participation from all five campuses increases the level of interest by broadening the issues beyond the individual or his or her department. Consortium-wide participation also creates a network of colleagues who serve as resources for each other long after the session has been completed.

What We Have Learned

The review of Five Colleges, Incorporated concluded with a national conference, "Cultures of Cooperation," that brought together presidents, provosts, deans, treasurers, and consortium directors. (The conference proceedings are available from Five Colleges, Incorporated.) During that conference, as during the review itself, the issue of assessment was raised many times. No single evaluation tool emerged that could be used to judge the worth of consortia, although there was unanimous agreement among the participants and speakers that assessment, including supporting data, is essential.

What did emerge were several recommendations as well as observations on what contributes to the success, or failure, of consortia. One suggestion was that in order to sustain the vitality of a consortium, to ensure that the consortium does not become mired in sponsoring programs that have grown stale or obsolete, cooperative programs should undergo periodic reviews to test their continuing effectiveness and importance to the institutions. Roger Clark, former director of the Committee on Institutional Cooperation (CIC), reported that the CIC builds in sunset clauses, ensuring that no program will continue without evaluating its usefulness and its costs to the institutions. Five Colleges has since inaugurated a five-year review for all cooperative programs. Academic program reviews are submitted to the deans' council and administrative programs to the chief financial officers. In addition, all Five College–funded activities, including faculty seminars, must submit an annual report indicating the number of events they sponsored that year and the number of faculty, students, or staff who participated.

Finally, we learned that criteria for success are generally held in common by most consortia, regardless of their size, membership, specific mission, or geographical location. A consortium is most successful when it provides opportunities for sharing that allow some financial relief—if not in cost savings, at least in cost avoidance. A consortium is financially successful when it provides additional benefits and services—to the institution, the faculty, students, and staff—that would otherwise be unavailable. A consortium succeeds when it shows respect for institutional differences even as it unites those institutions in mutually beneficial common efforts. A consortium serves its member institutions best when it does not stagnate, when it continues to offer flexibility and innovation, when it advances the possibility to experiment, to take risks, when it "challenges us all to do things differently. And that is valuable in and of itself." (Ruth Simmons, 1999).

References

Five Colleges, Incorporated. *Report of the Five College Long Range Planning Committee.* Amherst, Mass.: Five Colleges, Incorporated, 1981.
Simmons, R. Conference on Cultures of Cooperation. Nov. 13, 1999.

LORNA M. PETERSON *is executive director of Five Colleges, Incorporated in Amherst, Massachusetts.*

INDEX

Academic snobbery, 34–35
Adam's Chronicles, 99
Advisement, cooperative, 74–75
Agility, 91–92, 97
Agricultural extension, 21–22
Albany College of Pharmacy, 7
Albany Law School, 7
Albany Medical College, 7
Alberico, R., 63, 72
"Aligning for Shared Success" seminars, 4
Allen, B. M., 64, 71
Alliance for Higher Education, 12
American Chemical Society journals, 65
American Council on Education (ACE), 5
American Online Time Warner, 21
Americanization, 90
Amherst College, 12, 107. *See also* Five Colleges, Inc.
Anderson, D., 50
Anderson, W., 47, 54, 97–98
Applied research, 21–22
Archaeology education, technology in, 50–51
Arts education, 16, 50
Ascent of Man, The, 99
Assessment, of consortium effectiveness, 107–114
Associated Colleges of Central Kansas, 17
Associated Colleges of Illinois, 17
Associated Colleges of the Midwest (ACM), 55–62; Academic Collaboration grant of, 60–61; consortial issues in, 61–62; faculty development and collaboration in, 55–62; Global Partners Project of, 55, 56–58, 61, 93–94; Information Literacy Project of, 58–60; organization and funding of, 55–56
Associated Colleges of the South (ACS), 47–53, 97; Global Partners Project and, 55, 93–94; lessons learned in, 51–53; Technology Center of, 48, 51; technology partnerships of, 48–53
Associated Colleges of the St. Lawrence Valley (ACSLV), 3, 4–6; curricular

resources leveraging of, 7; human resources leveraging of, 4–6; Web site of, 17
Association for Consortium Leadership, 1–2, 18; directory of, 12; Web site of, 2
Association Liaison Office for the University Cooperation in Development (ALO), 95, 97
Association of Governing Boards, 22, 28
Association of Independent Kentucky Colleges and Universities, 17
Association of the United States Army, 78–79
Atlanta University Center, 17
Autonomous University of Queretaro, 96

Baird, L. L., 30, 36
Ball State University, 95
Basic School Eastern Consortia, 24
Best practices sharing, interinstitutional, 52
Birchard, K., 96, 98
Birmingham Area Consortium for Higher Education, 94
Birmingham-Southern College, 50
Bishop, J. E., 81, 88
Blackboard software, 42, 43
Blue Ridge Community College, 24, 26
Blue Ridge mountains area, 31. *See also* Leadership Jackson
Bonefas, S., 47, 54
Boyer, E. L., 24, 27–28, 28
Brazil, 94–95
Businesses: in public school-higher education consortia, 14; strategic alliances with, 19–28. *See also* Economic development partnerships
Butler University, 95

Cable television. *See* Television education
Canada, 97
Canadian National Site Licensing Project, 66
Canton College of Technology, 74, 75, 79
Capital Community College, 12

NEW DIRECTIONS FOR HIGHER EDUCATION IS NOW AVAILABLE ONLINE AT WILEY INTERSCIENCE

What is Wiley InterScience?

Wiley InterScience is the dynamic online content service from John Wiley & Sons delivering the full text of over 300 leading scientific, technical, medical, and professional journals, plus major reference works, the acclaimed *Current Protocols* laboratory manuals, and even the full text of select Wiley print books online.

What are some special features of Wiley InterScience?

Wiley InterScience Alerts is a service that delivers table of contents via e-mail for any journal available on Wiley InterScience as soon as a new issue is published online.
Early View is Wiley's exclusive service presenting individual articles online as soon as they are ready, even before the release of the compiled print issue. These articles are complete, peer-reviewed, and citable.
CrossRef is the innovative multi-publisher reference linking system enabling readers to move seamlessly from a reference in a journal article to the cited publication, typically located on a different server and published by a different publisher.

How can I access Wiley InterScience?

Visit http://www.interscience.wiley.com

Guest Users can browse Wiley InterScience for unrestricted access to journal Tables of Contents and Article Abstracts, or use the powerful search engine.
Registered Users are provided with a *Personal Home Page* to store and manage customized alerts, searches, and links to favorite journals and articles. Additionally, Registered Users can view free Online Sample Issues and preview selected material from major reference works.
Licensed Customers are entitled to access full-text journal articles in PDF, with select journals also offering full-text HTML.

How do I become an Authorized User?

Authorized Users are individuals authorized by a paying Customer to have access to the journals in Wiley InterScience. For example, a university that subscribes to Wiley journals is considered to be the Customer. Faculty, staff and students authorized by the university to have access to those journals in Wiley InterScience are Authorized Users. Users should contact their Library for information on which Wiley journals they have access to in Wiley InterScience.

ASK YOUR INSTITUTION ABOUT WILEY INTERSCIENCE TODAY!

HE108   Promising Practices in Recruitment, Remediation, and Retention
        Gerald H. Gaither
        Identifies the best practices for recruitment, remediation, and retention,
        describing lessons learned from innovative and successful programs across
        the nation, and shows how to adapt these efforts to today's diverse
        populations and technological possibilities.
        ISBN: 0-7879-4860-8

HE107   Roles and Responsibilities of the Chief Financial Officer
        Lucie Lapovsky, Mary P. McKeoan-Moak
        Offers strategies for balancing the operating and capital budgets,
        maximizing net enrollment revenues, containing costs, planning for the
        resource needs of technology, identifying and managing risks, and
        investing the endowment wisely.
        ISBN: 0-7879-4859-4

HE106   Best Practices in Higher Education Consortia: How Institutions Can Work
        Together
        Lawrence G. Dotolo, Jean T. Strandness
        Gives detailed accounts of activities and programs that existing consortia have
        already refined, providing practical models that can be replicated or modified
        by other institutions, and describes how to start and sustain a consortium.
        ISBN: 0-7879-4858-6

HE105   Reconceptualizing the Collegiate Ideal
        J. Douglas Toma, Adrianna J. Kezar
        Explores how administration, student affairs, and faculty work can work
        together to redefine the collegiate ideal, incorporating the developmental
        needs of a diverse student body and the changes in higher education's
        delivery and purpose.
        ISBN: 0-7879-4857-8

HE104   The Growing Use of Part-Time Faculty: Understanding the Causes
        and Effects
        David W. Leslie
        Presents analyses of the changes in academic work, in faculty careers, and in
        the economic conditions in higher education that are associated with the
        shift away from full-time academic jobs. Issues for research, policy, and
        practices are also discussed.
        ISBN: 0-7879-4249-9

HE103   Enhancing Productivity: Administrative, Instructional, and Technological
        Strategies
        James E. Groccia, Judith E. Miller
        Presents a multi-faceted approach for enhancing productivity that
        emphasizes both cost-effectiveness and the importance of bringing together
        all segments of the educational economy—institutions, faculty, students, and
        society—to achieve long-term productivity gains.
        ISBN: 0-7879-4248-0

HE102   Minority-Serving Institutions: Distinct Purposes, Common Goals
        Jamie P. Merisotis, Colleen T. O'Brien
        Serves as a primer on the growing group of minority-serving institutions,
        with the goal of educating leaders at mainstream institutions, analysts, and

those at minority-serving institutions themselves about their distinct purposes and common goals.
ISBN: 0-7879-4246-4

HE101 **The Experience of Being in Graduate School: An Exploration**
Melissa S. Anderson
Addresses the graduate experience from the standpoint of the students themselves. Presents what students have reported about their experience through interviews, surveys, ongoing discussions, and autobiographies.
ISBN: 0-7879-4247-2

HE99 **Rethinking the Dissertation Process: Tackling Personal and Institutional Obstacles**
Lester F. Goodchild, Kathy E. Green, Elinor L. Katz, Raymond C. Kluever
Identifies the institutional patterns and support structures that enhance the dissertation process, and describes how the introduction of dissertation-stage financial support and workshops can quicken completion rates.
ISBN: 0-7879-9889-3

HE98 **The Professional School Dean: Meeting the Leadership Challenges**
Michael J. Austin, Frederick L. Ahearn, Richard A. English
Focuses on the demanding leadership roles assumed by deans of social work, law, engineering, nursing, and divinity, providing case illustrations that illuminate the deanship experience at other professional schools.
ISBN: 0-7879-9849-4

HE97 **The University's Role in Economic Development: From Research to Outreach**
James P. Pappas
Offers models the academy can use to foster the ability to harness the research and educational resources of higher education institutions as well as the potential of state and land-grant universities to provide direct services for local and regional economic development through outreach missions.
ISBN: 0-7879-9890-7

HE96 **Preparing Competent College Graduates: Setting New and Higher Expectations for Student Learning**
Elizabeth A. Jones
Using the results of a nationwide study, this volume identifies specific ways institutions can help undergraduates attain the advanced thinking, communication, and problem-solving skills needed in today's society and workplace.
ISBN: 0-7879-9823-0

HE95 **An Administrator's Guide for Responding to Campus Crime: From Prevention to Liability**
Richard Fossey, Michael Clay Smith
Provides advice on crime prevention programs, campus police training, rape prevention, fraud in federal grant programs, and the problems associated with admitting students with criminal backgrounds.
ISBN: 0-7879-9873-7

HE115 Technology Leadership: Communication and Information Systems in Higher Education
George R. Maughan
Decisions about investments in information system infrastructure are among the most important—and costly—decisions campus and system administrators make. A wide variety of needs must be accommodated: those of students, faculty, and administrators themselves. This volume will help mainstream administrators think through the decision making process.
ISBN: 0-7879-5783-6

HE114 Developing and Implementing Service-Learning Programs
Mark Canada, Bruce W. Speck
Examines service learning—education that brings together students, teachers, and community partners in ways that foster the student's responsible citizenship and promotes a lifelong involvement in civic and social issues.
ISBN: 0-7879-5782-8

HE113 How Accreditation Influences Assessment
James L. Ratcliff, Edward S. Lubinescu, Maureen A. Gaffney
Examples of working programs include new methods of distance-education program assessment, an institutional accreditation self-study at the University of Vermont, and the Urban Universities Portfolio Project.
ISBN: 0-7879-5436-5

HE112 Understanding the Role of Public Policy Centers and Institutes in Fostering University-Government Partnerships
Lynn H. Leverty, David R. Colburn
Examines innovative approaches to developing the structure of programs in both traditional academic environments and in applied research and training; attracting and rewarding faculty engaged in public service; and determining which policy issues to approach at institutional levels.
ISBN: 0-7879-5556-6

HE111 Understanding the Work and Career Paths of Midlevel Administrators
Linda K. Johnsrud, Vicki J. Rosser
Provides information to help institutions develop recruitment efforts to fill midlevel administration positions and enlighten individuals about career possibilities in midlevel administration.
ISBN: 0-7879-5435-7

HE110 Moving Beyond the Gap Between Research and Practice in Higher Education
Adrianna Kezar, Peter Eckel
Provides suggestions for overcoming the research-practice dichotomy, such as creating a learning community that involves all the stakeholders, and using campus reading groups to help practitioners engage with scholarship.
ISBN: 0-7879-5434-9

HE109 Involving Commuter Students in Learning
Barbara Jacoby
Provides ways to create communities that meet the needs of students who live off-campus—from building a sense of community within individual courses to the creative use of physical space, information technology, living-learning communities, and experiential education programs.
ISBN: 0-7879-5340-7

Back Issue/Subscription Order Form

Copy or detach and send to:

Jossey-Bass, A Wiley Company, 989 Market Street, San Francisco CA 94103-1741

Call or fax toll-free: Phone 888-378-2537 6:30AM – 3PM PST; Fax 888-481-2665

Back Issues: Please send me the following issues at $27 each
(Important: please include series abbreviation and issue number.
For example EV93)

_____

_____

_____

$ _____   Total for single issues

$ _____   SHIPPING CHARGES: SURFACE   Domestic   Canadian

	First Item	$5.00	$6.00
	Each Add'l Item	$3.00	$1.50

For next-day and second-day delivery rates, call the number listed above.

Subscriptions: Please _start _renew my subscription to *New Directions for Higher Education* for the year 2____at the following rate:

U.S.	_ Individual $70		_ Institutional $145
Canada	_ Individual $70		_ Institutional $185
All Others	_ Individual $94		_ Institutional $219
Online Subscription			_ Institutional $145

**For more information about online subscriptions visit
www.interscience.wiley.com**

$ _____   Total single issues and subscriptions (Add appropriate sales tax for your state for single issue orders. No sales tax for U.S. subscriptions. Canadian residents, add GST for subscriptions and single issues.)

_ Payment enclosed (U.S. check or money order only)
_ VISA _MC _AmEx _Discover Card #_____ Exp. Date _____

Signature _____ Day Phone _____
_ Bill Me (U.S. institutional orders only. Purchase order required.)

Purchase order # _____
Federal Tax ID13559302   **GST 89102 8052**

Name _____

Address _____

_____

Phone _____ E-mail _____

For more information about Jossey-Bass, visit our Web site at www.josseybass.com

PROMOTION CODE ND03